N E R D
KNOW-HOW

N E R D
KNOW-HOW

· ·

The Best 27+ Apps for Work
& How to Use 'Em!

by Beth Ziesenis
Your Nerdy Best Friend

Avenue Z, Inc.
5694 Mission Center Road, Suite 602-111
San Diego, CA 92108
yournerdybestfriend.com

My mother
never had a Facebook page,
refused to use a smartphone,
rarely returned an email
and thought I was a hacker.

She once left me a voicemail:
"Your father says that
a hashtag is a pound sign.
We wait to hear from you."

But she was the best mom
a nerd could ever have.

We miss you, Mom.

Dedicated to Betty Bailey Ziesenis
February 8, 1945-April 21, 2014

Acknowledgements

Shout Outs

I'm grateful for the support of so many, especially the members of the NerdHerd (Page ix), who backed the book on Kickstarter.

Here are a few more folks who deserve special mention...

- She who figured out where all the little nerd cartoons would go:
  Designer Marian Hartsough

- She who found the typos:
  Editor Jeanne Marie Tokunaga

- She who kept my business going while I focused on the book:
  Assistant Molly Gardner

- He who won the 99designs book cover contest:
  Designer Sherwin Soy

- He who put up with my histrionics as I stressed out over the book:
  Husband D.J. Rausa

  (Honorable mention in this category goes to my dad and sister, Scott and Sarah Ziesenis.)

- The cool kids who let me sit at their table and gave me professional and personal support:
  The XY group of the National Speakers Association

Special Thanks to the NerdHerd!

Aaron Frazin

Aaron P. Hernandez

AAST

Addison & Ashley Simon

Aleks Jhun

Alia Snyder

Amanda White

AMC - Association Management Consultants, LLC

American Mensa

Amy Aschenbrenner

Amy Hilson

Amy Strasner

Anne Lupkoski

Art Herman

Ashley Kowal

Association Headquarters

Association Resources, Inc.

ASVMAE

Audrey Tweed-McCord, CAP

Barb David

Barbara ER Lucas

Beth Bridges

Beth Surmont, CMP

Brad Campbell

Brett M. Hanft CBA

Bruce R. Partain, CCE

Carol Ingram

Carol L. Lane

Carolina Wilson

Carrier Enterprise

Catherine Wells Bentz

Chad Ryg

Chris Davis

Chris Lyles

Christine Grove

Christine Wolf

Christy Mezei-Aurigemma

Clark Jones, REALTOR®, CRS, CRB, e-Pro, GRI, MRP, SRS

Colette Carlson

Cory Davis

Crystal Washington

D. Miracle

Dana Murphy-Love

Danielle Howell

Danya Hodgetts

Dawn James

Debbi Haddaway

Deloris Green Gaines

Denise M. Gilmore

Denise M. Smith

Dennis D. Sailer

Desert Belle Tour Boat

Di Richards

Diane Hanel, CAP

Diane Hohnstein

Diane Sullivan

Don Pendley

Donna Kendrena, CAP-OM

E. Milstone

Ed Weaver

Eileen Blake

Elena Gerstmann

Elizabeth B. Armstrong, CAE

Emily Arrowsmith, CAP-OM

Emily Waldrop

Eric H. Von Kaenel

Fazio International Ltd.

Francine Butler

Frontline Association
   Management

Gary Rifkin

Gianna Caruso

Gina Sutherland

Glen Cantrell

Gloria Rossiter, CAP-OM

Gregory M. Horine

Heather Kinney

Heather Rae Osborne

Holly Cormier

Hospitality Financial &
   Technology Professionals

Ian Roxburgh

Illinois Society of Association
   Executives

In-Joy Travel

Institute of Public Works
   Engineering Australasia

J-C Kortleven

Jack & Johnny Kabel

Jamie Buck

Jamison & Ashton

Jan Leighton

Janet McEwen, M.A., CAE

Jeff De Cagna

Jeffrey A. Horn, MPA

Jennifer Jones

Jerry Huffman

Jill Teter

Jim Rider

Joan Dankert

Joan Eisenstodt

Joan Teeling, CAP

Joanne Campbell

Jocelyn Boland

Jodi Ray

Joe Ferri

Joel Heffner

Special Thanks to the NerdHerd!

John Segota
John Tolson
Jon Rollefson
Jonathan Langham
Joy L. Goodrum
Joyce O'Brien
Julia D. McGann
Julie Fosgate
Julie McDade
Karen Clark
Karen Holt Peterson
Karoline Fritz
Karyn Keith
Kate Hunt
Kathleen Fitzpatrick
Kathleen Wilson, CAE
Kathryn Giblin
Kathy Newton
Katie Ryan-Anderson
Keely Yates
Kelly Burchfield
Kerri Wilson
Kim Williams
Kimberly J. Chatak-Nelson,
　CAP-OM
Kimberly Lilley, CIRMS, CMCA
Kris Finger
Laguna Beach Water District
Leadership Solutions
　International
Leigh Ann Senoussi

Liliana Donatelli
Linda Chreno
Linda Whale de Vargas
Lisa M. Prats, CAE
Lisa ONeill
Lisa Perry
Lissa Clayborn
Liz Hayes Hoffswell
Loretta Peskin
Lori A. Ropa, CAE
Lowell Aplebaum
Lucien Cloutier
Lynda Jennings
Marla Dalton, CAE
Mary Byers, CAE
Mary Kelly, PhD, CSP,
　Commander, USN (ret)
Matoka Snuggs
Melinda Buckley
Melissa G. Malechek, IOM
Melissa Heeke, CAE
Michael Anderson
Michael Shaw
Michael Weinberg
Michalia Gorden
Michele Huber
Michelle McMurtry
Monica J. McCorkle
Myra Casillas
Nanci McMaken
Nancy Grubb

Nancy McCulley
Nancy Phillips
Neal Klabunde
Nell Withers McCauley
Niagara Falls Tourism
Nora Y. Onishi
Oregon Society of Association
   Management
Patricia Wright
Patrick Dorsey
Patti Lawton
Pearl Amos
PHCC Educational Foundation
Phil Gerbyshak
Phyllis Bartosh
Polly Karpowicz
Ragan LeBlanc
Raquel M. Ortiz
Raymond J. White III
Renee A. Butler
Rita Tayenaka
Robert
Roberta Scarrow
Robin O. Brown
Roki Vargas
Ruth Neal
Samantha Greasley
Sara Miller
Sarah Martis, CAE
Scott Ziesenis, aka Papa
Sharmaine Battaglia Hamilton

Shawn Powelson
Sherri Starkey
Sierra Modro
Smokin' Joe and Marie Rausa
Society for College & University
   Planning
Stacie Swartzbaugh
Steve Brink
Stuart Sweeney
Sunset Breeze Real Estate
Susan Gauthier
Susan Klemmer
Susan Patereau
T. Hofmann
Tami DuBose
Terry Eichel
Terry Murphy, CRB, CRS, RCE
The Guy Beth Sleeps With
The Honorable Eric Witmayer
The Social Being
TheWellnessSisters.com
Thom Singer
Thomas N. Wright, CAE
Thomas W. Jackson
Tim & Shana Teehan
Tina Baldwin, CMCA, AMS
Todd Darian Shaffer, MD, MBA
Trips Unlimited
Truls Bjørvik
Wanda Furgason
Wayne King

Table of Contents

Table of Contents

Read This First. No, Really.

Introduction

Should You Use the Specific Tools in This Book?

The other day I was having a discussion with a fellow nerdy speaker/consultant. Roger Courville is THE guy when it comes to webinars and webcasting. Not only does he give presentations about webinar best practices (and more), he also consults with businesses and organizations about which tools will be the best for their virtual meeting needs.

Roger told me that he very purposefully avoids recommending individual tech tools because every need is different. For one organization, Zoom (Page 67) might be the perfect answer. Another group may need WebEx (Page 73). Someone else may be able to use the free version of AnyMeeting or the deluxe level of GoToWebinar. Roger says he doesn't feel comfortable to write a blog post that says, "Use this one."

Am I Doing Right by You Guys?

In my books and programs. I stand and say, "Oh my gosh! Zoom changed my world!" Or I tout LastPass (Page 33) as the solution to your password management issues. After my discussion with Roger, I asked myself if I was doing a disservice to my readers by focusing on the benefits of one tool rather than talking more generally about the category of tech tools then mentioning several.

Seth Godin Gave Me Confidence

When I was analyzing my philosophy about recommendations, a post from Seth Godin hit my inbox. Seth talked about not being afraid of making recommendations. Sure, my recommendations are my opinions, but I consider them very thoughtful opinions. I research everything I mention. Most of the tools I share are ones I use all the time. I am not paid by any tech company to mention a product, and I do not use affiliate links to get kickbacks if you sign up to use one.

The Best Way to Use This Book

My hope is that you read my books and leave my sessions with the idea that the tech world is full of amazing tools that you can start using right away. Maybe you start using Zoom (Page 67) for your videoconferences but then you realize you need something more and search around to see what is out there. My recommendations should open your eyes to a mind-boggling world of technology you never knew existed.

When you read this book, keep these thoughts in mind:

- **These Tools Are a Starting Point**
  For the most part, each tool is just one option in a very crowded and competitive category. I included alternatives to each, but that list is just a starting place for a plethora of competitors.

- **These Tools Are Awesome**
  I chose these particular tools for their dependability, multi-platform availability, popularity and ease of use. If you've attended any of my presentations, this book serves as the missing manual for many of the tools I talk about.

Introduction

- **This Book Is a Starting Point**
  For each tool, you'll find insight, tips and ideas, but the sections are by no means exhaustive. If I covered all the functionality, each chapter would be a book by itself. The goal is to provide you some key techniques for making the most of the tool.

- **This Book Is Out of Date**
  We triple checked the pricing, platforms and functionality of the tools in this book right up until we pushed the print button, but the next week, the descriptions were out of date. Except for poor Tagxedo (Page 156), you can bet these tools will constantly evolve.

Look for changes in these areas:

- Platform availability (access via new operating systems, etc.)
- Pricing (up and down)
- Extra-special features (groundbreaking, oh-my-gosh functionality with big announcements)
- Integrations and partnerships (increasing every day)
- Incorporation into the Internet of Things, like IFTTT (Page 25) logging how many times your smart dishwasher runs or Evernote (Page 14) automatically sending new recipes to your smart stove

Despite these inevitable changes and advancements, you can be confident that this book will serve as the starting place for putting this technology into action for your work, home and life.

Organize

· ·

In this chapter:

PLUS

Dropbox

dropbox.com

● ●

I could not, would not, cannot live without **Dropbox**.

Well, perhaps I'm exaggerating a tad. I could probably survive without a robust cloud synchronization service like Dropbox, but I sure wouldn't want to. Dropbox is probably my preferred service in this very crowded category because I've been using it so long, but it's also arguably the biggest and most established service of this type.

In a nutshell, Dropbox is your hard drive—everywhere. When you sign up for an account, you download the software to your machine and install apps on your devices. The system creates a Dropbox folder on your computer, and anything you place into that folder is available anywhere you need it.

Dropbox Synchronization and Access

Once you've started populating files into the folder, Dropbox saves a local copy on your machine and creates another copy on one of its servers elsewhere (in the infamous cloud). When you make changes to a Dropbox file, your cloud version is instantly updated, and the new version is available wherever you access it.

You have a number of options for getting to your files from anywhere. You can access the files from your local drive even if you're not connected to the Internet. Once you connect again, everything is synchronized.

If you're on someone else's computer or device, you can log into your account on the Dropbox site. There your files are organized the same way they are on your computer, and you can easily search for what you need.

On mobile devices, when you're connected to the Internet, you have access to all your files. Files are not stored on your phone unless you choose to do so one by one.

Nerd Know-How:
Recover Earlier Versions of Files

If you overwrite an important document with the wrong changes, don't worry. Dropbox saves the previous versions for you for up to a month, so you can revert back or even restore deleted files.

Version history of 'Deep Dive Book July 2014.docx'

Dropbox keeps a snapshot every time you save a file. You can preview and restore 'Deep Dive Book July 2014.docx' by choosing one of the versions below:

Version 51 (current)	Edited by Beth Ziesenis (Beth's MacBook Pro)	Yesterday 6:37 PM	7.64 MB
Version 50	Edited by Beth Ziesenis (Beth's MacBook Pro)	Yesterday 6:04 PM	7.43 MB
Version 49	Edited by Beth Ziesenis (Beth's MacBook Pro)	Yesterday 4:47 PM	7.18 MB
Version 48	Edited by Beth Ziesenis (Beth's MacBook Pro)	Yesterday 4:43 PM	7.18 MB
Version 47	Edited by Beth Ziesenis (Beth's MacBook Pro)	Yesterday 4:43 PM	7.18 MB

Dropbox Version History

When I was working on my second book, I hired a guy to find logos for all the tools and store them in a Dropbox folder. I didn't touch the folder for a while; and when I finally needed them, OH MY GOSH! The files were gone! He had cleaned out his folder to save space.

Before I panicked—OK, maybe in the middle of a full-fledged panic—I was able to recover the deleted files through the Dropbox restore feature.

Dropbox Sharing

One of the best features of Dropbox and other cloud storage companies is the sharing option. Right click on any Dropbox file name, and you can get an instant link for access to a file or folder. You can give out the link to anyone you wish, and the recipients can view or download the file. This is a great way to transfer larger files without having to attach them to emails and clog up inboxes.

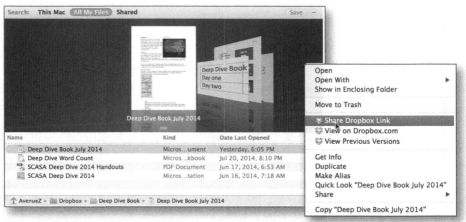

Dropbox Sharing Menu

Nerd Know-How:
Share Handouts in Dropbox

For every presentation, I create a super-secret Dropbox link for attendees. I drop any special graphics I've created for the group as well as a copy of the slides and my top 100 tech tools into a quick reference guide.

You can also share folders for collaboration. You can give members of a folder different permissions, meaning you can give one committee member read-only access and another access to edit and save changes.

A major drawback of Dropbox collaboration at the free and lower-priced levels is when two or more people are editing the same file at the same time. Instead of alerting you to other users, Dropbox saves a "conflicted copy" of each user's file. But if you spring for the Dropbox for Business level, a new feature lets you collaborate in real time through Microsoft Office documents. And in the spring of 2015, Dropbox announced a feature that lets you add comments on files. The comments are visible when you view the file online or on a device. You can use the "@" symbol to tag contacts or emails so collaborators get a note to review. This feature is helpful for passing around a document in the office to get feedback from everyone.

Dropbox Third-Party Integrations

Another feature of Dropbox that makes it super valuable is its integration with 300,000+ third-party apps. Most of them allow you to access Dropbox files directly or save documents into a Dropbox folder. Here are three super useful apps:

1. **Send to Dropbox**
   sendtodropbox.com
   Set up an email address that saves attachments into a Dropbox folder.

2. **DROPitTOme**
   dropittome.com
   Let others drop files into your Dropbox system with this free tool.

3. **IFTTT** (Page 25)
   ifttt.com
   Use IFTTT recipes to perform dozens of tasks with Dropbox behind the scenes for free.

Nerd Know-How: Replace Your PC

In late 2014, Dropbox and Microsoft Office teamed up so Dropbox users can edit in Office apps with just a click from their mobile devices. The Office apps are robust and full of features, just like their desktop counterparts, meaning that the Dropbox integration gives your mobile device almost all the power of full-fledged computers.

5 Things to Know About Dropbox

1. Dropbox is arguably the leader in cloud-based file synchronization.

2. With Dropbox, you can share files and folders instantly and invite others to collaborate, although if you don't have Dropbox for Business, you have to watch when more than one person is editing at a time because Dropbox will save separate "conflicted copies." A newer feature lets you add comments to Dropbox files for your collaborators.

3. Dropbox gives 2GB of storage for free, and you can earn up to 16GB by inviting colleagues and through other tasks. Paid versions start at $99 a year for 1TB of storage, which is a helluva lot.

4. Recent changes to Dropbox include faster uploads and synchronization for very large files, as well as instant camera uploads from mobile devices.

5. Third-party apps give Dropbox even more functionality and flexibility.

NerdHerd Thumbs Up: Dropbox is a favorite

It's no surprise that Dropbox wins props from several NerdHerders, including Amy Hilson and Dana Murphy-Love. Amy says, "Dropbox makes working from anywhere SO easy," and frequent traveler Dana adds that Dropbox allows access to documents easily, even without a VPN connection.

Dropbox Alternatives

The cloud-storage service field is very, very crowded; but a handful of companies lead the pack. Most of the major players in this field have many of the same characteristics and capabilities. Here's a summary of the features you'll find in most (if not all) of the top tools.

- Free storage of 2-15GB, with the capability to earn more when you spread the word
- Web and mobile apps to access your files from anywhere
- Real-time synchronization wherever the service is installed
- Capability to restore deleted files and older versions
- Collaboration via shared folders or files, sometimes with different levels of permissions
- Instant file and folder sharing via links
- Integration with third-party apps for enhanced features and accessibility

Top Alternatives

- **Box**
  box.com

  Box gives you 10GB with the free plan, but you'll have to pay extra for version tracking and some of the other features Dropbox gives away. Starting at $5 per user, you can start collaborating (but just between paid users). For $15 per user per month, you can enable project management with tasks and deadlines.

  A cool feature with Box is the built-in editing software. Box has its own software that lets you edit and create documents within the system, as well as through outside software such as Microsoft Office.

- **Google Drive**
  google.com/drive

  Google Drive gives you 15GB free with bonus space for smallish photos, though your storage is shared between your regular files as well as Gmail messages and attachments. 100GB will cost you just $24 a year. As one might expect, Google Drive integrates seamlessly with all things Google. You also have built-in software for editing and creating.

  One of Google Drive's coolest features is the real-time collaboration. If you have several committee members working on the same document at the same time, their words and changes appear on the screen, color-coded and even labeled with the users' names. Like Dropbox, Google Drive gives you the ability to revert to older versions of files.

I often ask my Fancy Hands assistants (Page 184) to use a Google Sheet to collect data, and sometimes I type them little messages while they're working away to freak them out. It's one of my small nerdy joys.

- **Microsoft OneDrive**
  onedrive.com

  OneDrive's primary purpose is to make it easy to store Microsoft documents when you have a Microsoft 365 subscription. Although anyone can get an account with 15GB of free storage or 100GB starting at $1.99 per month, if you're a subscriber, you get 1TB free.

  OneDrive lets users communicate in real time when they're in Microsoft Office documents. At least that's what the website says. I did an experiment, and it was a mess. Comments disappeared; access was denied; users got frustrated and turned to cupcakes. OneDrive has some improving to do.

- **Younity**
getyounity.com

 And now for something completely different. Younity bills itself as a "personal cloud." Your files are not stored or synched among your devices. Younity just gives you access to everything you share from your home base computer and any other connected computer. If you search for files with Younity, it'll look on every computer that is connected.

 Younity is perfect if you have a large music or video library on your home computer but don't want to take up space on your iPhone. Younity will connect to those files and stream them to your device.

 The cool thing is that the access is almost instant—there's no downloading or synching. But to get to your files from a remote site (any computer or Apple device), your connected computer has to be on. You can share files with Younity, but the links expire in a week.

NerdHerd Thumbs Up:
Google Drive is great for collaboration

Gina Sutherland loves that Google Drive allows real-time collaboration, but she also notes that the services keep growing. "Collaboration tools, forms, drawings . . .seems like there's something new every day." Neal Klabunde from Dirty Fingernails Marketing likes the Google Sheets program in the Google Drive suite because he can share documents across different devices.

Four Ways to Back Up Your Files

Although cloud storage services do keep a copy of your files on their servers, experts say you shouldn't rely on them as your backup system. For me this is a "do as they say, not as I do" thing because Dropbox is my backup plan. But you have plenty of cloud backup services to do the job.

For the online backup services, you generally set up an account; tell them which drives, folders and files to back up; and let them get to work. They can work in the background all the time or back up on a schedule. If your computer blows up, you can restore your files to another machine or recover an earlier version of a document.

1. **CrashPlan**
   code42.com/crashplan

   If I didn't use Dropbox for my backup plan, I'd choose CrashPlan. The free version, aptly named CrashPlan Free, puts the backup network into your hands by allowing you to connect to friends' computers for storage. You back up to someone else's computer while he stores his backup on yours. Neither one of you can see the other's files, but everyone has peace of mind— without a monthly subscription fee.

   Its paid versions are pretty comparable to other services— $59.99 a year for unlimited data from one computer. CrashPlan also offers to save multiple versions of your active files as well as all the files you delete. And you can back up to multiple locations, such as its online cloud, another computer and an external hard drive.

2. Carbonite and 3. Mozy
carbonite.com and **mozy.com**

Carbonite and Mozy have been around the longest and are perhaps the best known. They have a lot of similarities, so to me choosing one over the other is like choosing between McDonald's and Burger King. (I have a strong preference for Wendy's instead, but that's beside the point.) Carbonite looks great on paper—unlimited storage on unlimited devices for $59 a year. But if you read the small print, you'll soon discover that if you have more than 200GB to back up, your backups will be slower and take longer—data throttling, if you will. That said, it's a simple service with a great reputation; so if you don't need 200+GB, it's a nice option.

Mozy was the first online backup service I ever used, way back in the day when it would take f.o.r.e.v.e.r to update online. You can have 2GB for free, or choose a paid plan starting at $5.99 per month for up to 50GB. Both Carbonite and Mozy now offer file synchronization and sharing à la Dropbox.

4. SocialSafe
socialsafe.net

Are your tweets and Facebook posts works of art? SocialSafe (which seems to be rebranding as **digi.me**) can help you preserve them forever so your kids and grandkids have a permanent record of what you ate for breakfast every day and your reviews of local cupcake shops.

SocialSafe backs up the data from social media sites such as LinkedIn, Facebook and Instagram. The free version archives up to four sites, and starting at $6.99 a year, you can create PDFs of your archives and more.

When I first heard about this tool, I thought it was a nutty idea. Why would you need to keep a copy of your Facebook posts? And who wants to keep all the old tweets? But some high-profile hacks in the past couple of years brought all kinds of important questions into play. If Facebook fails, what happens to all the awesome photo albums you've created? And how can you get back all your LinkedIn contacts if the service blows up one day?

NerdHerd Thumbs Up: Carbonite provides access to files from mobile devices

Ed Weaver from B&D Technologies uses the Carbonite app because it lets him access, print and email all his backed-up files on the go.

Evernote

Picture your desk. Somewhere within reach is a thick manila folder. Inside you've gathered everything you need for a project: scraps of paper, sticky notes, printed web pages and emails, plus maybe a couple of photos.

Evernote is a digital copy of that folder everywhere, instantly synchronized wherever you access it and shareable with whoever needs it. I'll go out on a very safe limb here and say that Evernote is the king of notetaking and information organization apps. Since its release in 2008, it has grown exponentially and ubiquitously, gaining millions of loyal followers and creating integrations into dozens and dozens of other apps and programs.

Evernote lets you store pictures, documents, notes, webpages, snippets of text, handwritten doodles on napkins, emails and anything else you can possibly imagine. The search engine even combs text in pictures (and in PDFs for Premium subscribers).

You can add your information to Evernote in every possible way as well—through browser plug-ins, email, web apps, desktop apps and mobile apps. When you have the information you want, you can tag it, organize it into folders, share it and search for it.

NerdHerd Thumbs Up: EVERYONE loves Evernote

Evernote got the most mentions in the NerdHerd's favorite tool list. Here's why:

- Greg Horine loves that you can easily capture and retrieve all information.

- Danielle Howell uses Evernote to organize and search her files on the go.

- Jeffrey Horn keeps all his notes in Evernote and finds the system easy to search and organize from a variety of devices.

- Melissa Heeke creates notes and lists in the cloud.

- "Evernote organizes everything in my life!" says Polly Karpowicz. "It brings order to all bits and pieces of info that I come across for professional and personal use, and it makes it easy to save, organize and find later."

- John Segota and Raquel M. Ortiz both love it as well. Raquel says, "Evernote is the one place for many types of information, accessible anywhere I am from any device or computer." She's a law librarian, so she should know.

Ten Uses for Evernote

Type "uses for Evernote" into a search engine, and you'll find a kabillion lists of ways people use this flexible tool. Evernote works well for any type of information gathering and archiving. Here are just 10 ways to use it:

1. Save notes from office meetings to share with the team.

2. Create a master to-do list.

3. Sign up for newsletters with your unique Evernote email to collect them without clogging up your inbox.

4. Collect tech tools to try later.

5. Integrate with other services such as IFTTT (Page 25) to store photos, documents and more.

6. Keep critical information at the ready, such as credit card numbers and driver's license scans.

7. Create Notebooks for clients to store all their paperwork in one place.

8. Record a meeting or a note to yourself and add the audio.

9. Snap pictures of the whiteboard after a brainstorming session and let Evernote convert the picture into searchable text.

10. Digitize and organize your receipts.

Emailing Evernote Notes

Since I frequently receive cool tips from readers about new tech tools, email is one of my favorite methods for saving information. Evernote gives you a unique email address for notes. The key to keeping them organized is in the email subject line. The order is critical.

Here's the formula:

Email Subject: [Title of Note]
![Reminder Date] @[Notebook] #[Tag]

[Title of Note]
The first field is the name of the note.

![Reminder Date]
If you want to set a reminder to complete a task in a note, put an exclamation point in front of a date. Evernote will ask you if you want emails to remember your deadlines.

@[Notebook]
Evernote organizes itself in a number of ways, including Notebooks and tags. Think of the Notebook as the folder on your desk. Each note can be in only one Notebook, but it could have multiple tags. In your email subject line, use the @ sign in front of the Notebook name. **Tip:** An email won't create a new Notebook for you. Use the @ sign for an existing folder, or it will automatically be filed in the last Notebook you had open.

#[Tag]
Unlike Notebooks, you can add multiple tags to any note. For example you could put a new tech tool that you wanted to use for yourself in a personal Notebook with tags for #work and #productivity. Then you can sort by either of those tags to find all those notes if you decide you want to share that information with colleagues.

Here's an example of how Evernote would translate an email using the subject line. The subject line here was "New Apps @New Tools #tool lists."

New Apps @New Tools #tool lists

Beth Ziesenis <beth@y   12:21 PM (1 hour ago)
to Evernote

Here's a great list of new productivity apps from PC Magazine.

http://www.pcmag.com/article2/0,2817,2362574,00.asp

Evernote Email

Within 30 seconds of hitting the send button, here's how it ended up in Evernote:

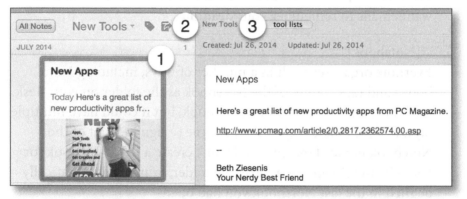

Evernote Entry After Email

1. The note was named "New Apps."

2. It was filed automatically in the "New Tools" Notebook.

3. Evernote automatically added the email note to the tags category called "tool lists."

Nerd Know-How:
Take Better Notes at Meetings

One of the best applications for Evernote is at business meetings. You can collect and tag all the information you'll need for a meeting so it's at the ready when you need to discuss it. You can also create action items and to-do lists to help follow up. And you can take meeting notes directly into Evernote or even snap a picture of the whiteboard to capture all the important points.

4 Things to Know About Evernote

1. Evernote is a note-taking tool that lets you organize every note, document, picture, audio file, web clipping and email that you may ever need into searchable, sharable Notebooks.

2. You can throw information you need to save into Evernote in almost any format from almost any device.

3. Evernote uses a system of Notebooks and tags to help you find and share the information you need in a jiffy.

4. The free version is great for a casual user, but you may need to upgrade to one of the two paid plans to take advantage of features such as business card processing and full-text PDF searching.

Nerd Know-How: Transcribe Business Cards

In 2014, LinkedIn killed CardMunch, an app that helped digitize business cards. The new solution, according to LinkedIn, was a partnership with Evernote. All I have to say is, "Meh," but to be fair, I say that about almost all business card scanner apps.

I tried several times to make the Evernote Business Card scanner work, but the results were inconsistent, as they are with most scanners. The inconsistency means that I have to scan one card, check/change the info and then go on to the next. All this checking and rechecking takes me longer than typing the card information. That's why I outsource my business card work to Fancy Hands (Page 184).

Evernote Alternatives

- **Microsoft OneNote**
  onenote.com

  Evernote competes directly with Microsoft's OneNote, which was a well-kept secret until Evernote became so popular. OneNote used to be an $80 stand-alone app that was included in the higher-priced MS Office suites. But Microsoft came out with a free version and now includes the paid version in MS Office 365 subscriptions.

  OneNote integrates very well with MS Office—no surprise there. OneNote and Evernote are organized slightly differently, but when you compare them side by side, they do about the same things. Which one you choose is just a matter of preference.

* **Notability** and **LectureNotes**
  gingerlabs.com and **acadoid.com**

  To replicate the nostalgic feeling of taking notes with pen and paper, a couple of tablet apps can help. The Notability iPad app combines handwritten or typed notes with audio recordings to help you truly capture the ideas of a meeting or brainstorming session. It synchronizes with Dropbox (Page 2) to save your notes for access anywhere. For Android tablets, you might try LectureNotes in conjunction with **LectureRecordings** or **LectureVideos** to sync notes and audio/video and export to Evernote. Both handwriting apps are helpful for marking up PDFs and other documents as well.

NerdHerd Thumbs Up:
AudioNote records meetings

"The older I get, the more tools I need to help me remember things," says Kathleen Wilson from NATLE. She uses AudioNote (luminantsoftware.com/iphone/audionote.html) to record meetings and synchronize her notes so she can participate more rather than focusing on taking minutes.

Four Bonus Evernote Products

1. **Skitch**
   evernote.com/skitch

   Skitch is Evernote's screencapture tool (see more screencapture tools, Page 78), and it makes itself even handier because it's also available as an app. Skitch lets you grab a screen from your computer or mobile device and add annotations and notes.

2. **Penultimate**
   evernote.com/penultimate

   I have crappy handwriting, so I don't know why I'd use this app to pretend my iPad is a notepad. But if you're more creative with a pen than a keyboard, this may be a useful app for you.

3. **Scannable**
   evernote.com/scannable

   Evernote recently released a new app to help users scan documents into the system more easily. Scannable also helps improve the efficiency of Evernote's system to manage business cards (Page 20).

4. **Evernote Food**
   evernote.com/food

   This app lets you take pictures of food and keep track of recipes. Since Evernote lets you organize things already, I don't know why you would need a separate program for food (and if I cooked, I'd probably collect mine on Pinterest). But I suppose if you're really scouring the world for creative cuisine and need a dedicated way to organize the recipes, here you go.

Four Tools to Organize Your Home

Evernote can organize every note in your life, but other specialty tools are built to keep other areas of your life neat and tidy.

1. **Bawte**
   bawte.com

   Do you have a drawer for all of your appliance manuals and registration forms (that you never send in)? Get rid of them all by signing up for Bawte, which keeps your appliances on file and hooks you up with the manuals and other paperwork in electronic format.

   NerdHerder Denise Smith tells us that Bawte helps her organize appliance warrantees and recall info with just a scan of the UPC code. "I don't need to keep all the owners' manuals and that means less clutter," Denise says.

2. **BrightNest**
   brightnest.com

   The site, powered by Angie's List, offers tips and life hacks, but the apps (Android and iOS) help you organize cleaning schedules, repair and maintain your appliances, and keep your home running smoothly. (If anyone could use a home cleaning tool, it's me—but I've yet to set up a BrightNest schedule. Go figure.)

3. **Know Your Stuff**
   knowyourstuff.org

   This free service helps you inventory your possessions, possibly avoiding an insurance battle after a disaster. The website is handy, but the apps have gotten horrible reviews for buggy-ness.

4. **Key Ring**
   keyringapp.com

   NerdHerder Veronica Morales from The Social Being likes to organize all her loyalty cards with Key Ring.

NerdHerd Thumbs Up: My Measures stores and shares dimensions

Eric H. Von Kaenal works with kitchen designers, and he uses My Measures (sis.si/my-measures) to snap a picture of an object and receive an instant analysis of the dimensions.

IFTTT

ifttt.com

Without even realizing it, you probably do the same tasks over and over—such as checking the weather, saving attachments from emails, tweeting your latest blog post on Twitter.

Though it takes just a few minutes to complete each task, these little jobs add up fast, and you probably have better uses of your time in today's crazy-busy lifestyle.

IFTTT, which stands for "if this then that," is one of a category of tools that will help you automate some of these little tasks so you don't have to think about them.

If This Then That

IFTTT can save you time, make you organized and generally rock your world—if you take the time to set up the recipes. The best news is that IFTTT users have already set up a ton of recipes for you, so all you have to do is use their genius with your account.

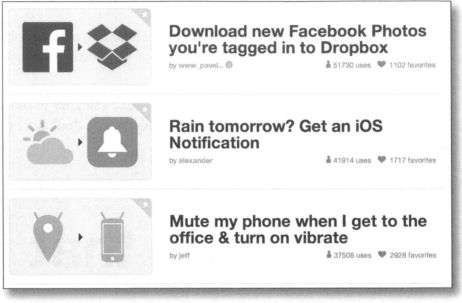

IFTTT Recipes

IFTTT works with a number of devices and gadgets, venturing into the world we know as "The Internet of Things." You can automate tasks with Nest thermostats, Philips Hue light bulbs and many fitness trackers. IFTTT's apps also create opportunities to use specific iOS and Android features, such as location tracking and selfies.

Organize

Many of the recipes have fine-tuning options to do exactly what you want, such as the recipe I have set up to create a blog post from videos I favorite on YouTube. You can set up a formula so that the title, description, tags and categories can all be personalized—either with text you type in or merged fields from the original video.

if You Tube **then** ⓦ

New favorite video by askbetnz   Create a post on your WordPress blog

Recipe Title

Publish YouTube to Your Nerdy Best Friend

use '#' to add tags

Action

Create a post
This Action will create a normal post on your WordPress blog.

ⓦ Title

Title   +

ⓦ Body

Description   EmbedCode   +

Some HTML ok

ⓦ Categories

Comma separated   +

ⓦ Tags

video,   +

Comma seperated

ⓦ Post status

Save as draft

Update

YouTube to WordPress Post

27

The only bummer about the Do apps is that each one only handles three tasks, which means you're getting just nine total buttons that take up three app spaces of real estate on your phone.

Nerd Know-How: Do More with IFTTT's Do Apps

Nerds like me take the time to root out and create IFTTT recipes to automate our most tiresome tasks, but the setup can be time consuming and annoying. In early 2015 IFTTT updated its mobile app to the hipper-titled IF and added three new apps in the process. **Do Camera**, **Do Note** and **Do Button** make it even easier to create recipes with a wizard approach that takes you through clear steps to create shortcuts that do what you need. My favorite shortcut is in Do Button: You can create a button that will fake an incoming phone call so you can get out of a meeting. "Oh, excuse me. I have to get this . . ." Do Camera has another handy task—the ability to take a handful of pictures and create a GIF.

Organize

Here are a few other recipes you may find useful.

Five IFTTT Recipe Ideas for Social Media

1. When I change my Facebook profile picture, update my Twitter picture.
2. Back up images from Pinterest to Dropbox.
3. When I'm tagged in a Facebook picture, save it to Google Drive.
4. When I tweet something on Twitter, post it to LinkedIn.
5. When I favorite a video on YouTube, publish it to my WordPress blog.

Five IFTTT Recipes for Organization

1. Automatically upload all my Gmail attachments to Dropbox.
2. Unmute my phone when I get home, and mute my ringer at bedtime.
3. Send phone screenshots to Evernote.
4. File sales receipts I receive via email into a Google spreadsheet.
5. Download all my phone contacts to a Google spreadsheet.

Five IFTTT Recipes for Home

1. Text someone I love when I leave work.
2. Get an email when the forecast calls for rain.
3. Track my Fitbit sleep logs in a Google spreadsheet.
4. When my Jawbone UP device registers that I am waking up, adjust my Philips Hue light bulb to simulate daybreak.
5. If I don't work out for three days, email me that picture of me with too many chins.

4 Things to Know About IFTTT

1. IFTTT automates tasks with cloud-based services and high-tech gadgets.

2. Start by browsing the existing recipes to get an idea of what types of things IFTTT can do. Use the Do apps on your devices for quick actions, or develop your own recipes.

3. IFTTT is free, which is amazing. I expect the company may look into paid levels in the future.

4. As our world creates more ways to integrate daily tasks into technology, look for more IFTTT recipes to pull all these services together.

IFTTT Alternatives

- **Zapier**
  zapier.com

  IFTTT lists less than 200 apps and services; Zapier has more than twice that. Zapier's free version gives you five "Zaps" (recipes) with a total of 80 tasks a month. When you upgrade to a paid plan (starting at $20 a month), you can have more Zaps and access the premium connections.

- **Wappwolf**
  wappwolf.com

  This tool has a wacky, weird name; but it can be pretty handy. Wappwolf focuses on automations for three cloud services: Dropbox, Box, and Google Drive (See discussion of all three starting on Page 8). The types of automations are pretty cool, such as the ability to convert pictures placed into a certain folder into gray scale or add a logo. Premium plans start at $5 a month and include advanced capabilities such as converting a document to an eBook.

Five Social Media Automation Tools

IFTTT excels at social media automation, but so do these apps and services.

1. **Buffer**
   bufferapp.com

   Buffer has made quite a splash in the social media management category. The free version lets you schedule up to 10 posts in advance per social account (Facebook, Twitter, Google+, LinkedIn, App.net). If you have more than one social account per platform (like two Facebook pages), prices start at $10 a month. The paid plans have a handy RSS feed system that lets you see content from your favorite sites while you're scheduling posts inside the app or on the site.

2. **Hootsuite**
   hootsuite.com

   Hootsuite is arguably the mother of all social media management tools. It allows you to manage your accounts and schedule your social media updates with ease. The free version is pretty skimpy these days; but starting at $9.99 a month, you can get advanced features such as up to 50 social profiles, enhanced statistics, and bulk message scheduling of up to 350 posts at a time.

3. **TweetDeck**
   tweetdeck.twitter.com

   In 2013 Twitter killed the app versions of this tool, but the web-based services still rock. You can monitor multiple Twitter feeds, get alerts for content, schedule tweets in advance and log in with multiple accounts. If you want to integrate TweetDeck with other social media options, you can use IFTTT (Page 25) to set up recipes to repost tweets elsewhere.

NerdHerder Joel Heffner uses Twitter as a place to connect with his favorite contacts, and Shana Teehan uses TweetDeck to manage multiple Twitter accounts. "As a communications director, TweetDeck allows me to actually take nights and weekends off," Shana says.

4. **Swayy**
   swayy.co

   This 2014 tool is a very smart way to discover and curate your social media content. Swayy analyzes your social media accounts, looking at both what you share and the content that your followers prefer, plus other topics you add. Then the service brings the content to you, either via email or the site. You can share the content with just a click.

5. **Triberr**
   triberr.com

   My speaking buddy Phil Gerbyshak set up a Triberr account for members of the XY speakers' group (named for the generations of our members). We see the brilliant posts of our colleagues; and by rolling our mouse over the share button (no clicking needed!), we can share members' posts with our networks. This is a great resource for like-minded bloggers and content curators, not only for helping members find great content but also for helping each blogger get a little more reach.

LastPass   lastpass.com

Gulp. Here's a graphic of a few of the major security breaches of the past five years. Scary isn't it?

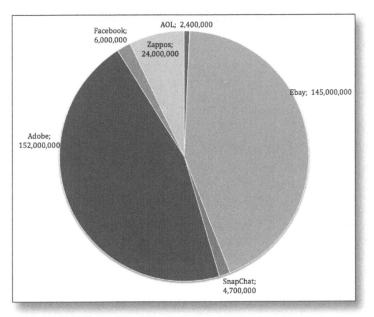

Major Security Breaches

One of the most common online security mistakes we make, besides picking passwords that are too easy, is using the same password for multiple sites. Many of us have two passwords: a short and easy one for everyday sites, like when a site says, "Register Now to Get the White Paper." And then we have a longer password—maybe with some numbers in it—for our "serious" sites.

The bad guys know this, and when they hack into a site, they get our username/password combos and try them on other sites and eventually get to some pretty valuable information.

It's time to truly take charge of your password and Internet security issues. **LastPass** is a free, cloud-based tool that allows you to create one master password to gain access to all your sites. Further, I love that as soon as you install it, it scrapes all the sites in your browser history to show you just how many you have and how vulnerable you really are.

The magic button is the Security Challenge. Within minutes, LastPass gathers all your usernames and passwords and gives you a grade.

LastPass Security Challenge

Once you run the security challenge, LastPass will give you a list of all the duplicate passwords and vulnerable sites. In late 2014, LastPass and a couple of other major password managers added functionality that will make it easier to change passwords on multiple sites in one sitting if there's a major breach like the Heartbleed bug.

After you complete the Security Challenge, LastPass stores all the user-names and passwords it discovered in a vault. You access your entries via one giant password—the last password you'll ever need. (LastPass—get it?) When you visit a page while you're logged into LastPass via browser plug-ins, LastPass will fill in your username/password automatically, letting you choose among logins if you have multiple accounts, like my Twitter personas.

Your LastPass vault is searchable; and you can organize passwords by function, such as personal passwords or work passwords.

LastPass Login

Nerd Know-How: Share Passwords Safely

One of my favorite LastPass features is the ability to share passwords with others without giving up security. Just enter the email that your contact uses to sign in to her LastPass account, and your contact can use your credentials to log into your accounts without access to the actual password. This prevents those dangerous conversations that start, "Just log in as me ..."

Share LastPass Password

It's a little disconcerting to put everything in LastPass' hands, but CNET, PCWorld, Consumer Reports and Lifehacker all give it thumbs up. That being said, LastPass received negative press in 2014 for not disclosing a minor breach a year before.

Nerd Know-How: Prepare for the New World of Digital Security

We already have switched from passwords to fingerprints, and the next level of password security could be just a heartbeat away, literally. Stay tuned for wearable technology that monitors your heartbeat and other bodily cues to identify you and release your passwords. A team at UC Berkeley's School of Information is even working on wearable technology that will read your brainwaves so you can think your password to get into a site. Creepy or awesome? Can't we have both?

5 Things to Know About LastPass

1. LastPass is a password manager that lets you generate unique, very complicated passwords for every site you visit then makes them accessible so you never have to remember them.

2. With one click of the "Security Challenge" button, the system discovers all your username/password combos and keeps them locked away in a vault so you can use them from anywhere.

3. The upgrade ($12 a year) allows you to manage your passwords on mobile devices. On the latest models of iPhone, you can use Touch ID to safeguard your passwords with fingerprint technology.

4. No online service is 100% safe, but sites such as LastPass take drastic measures to safeguard data—much more than the sticky-note collection around your computer monitor.

5. You can share your usernames and passwords with colleagues through the system so your information is more secure.

NerdHerd Thumbs Up: LastPass saves time

Both Carolina Wilson and Kim Robinson make use of LastPass. "It's completely automated," Kim says. "I only have to remember one master password, and it works across devices and platforms."

LastPass Alternatives

- **KeePass**
  keepass.info

  KeePass is an open-source program that you download or store on a USB drive. KeePass stores all your information locally by default, so if you're worried about the security of the cloud, this could be an option. It was built for Windows, but there are ways to use it on other platforms. I can't bring myself to use KeePass because it seems to be one "p" short of a socially acceptable name: I keep reading it as "Keep-ass." That's just wrong.

- **1Password**
  agilebits.com/onepassword

  Unlike the other password managers on this list, 1Password doesn't have a free version; and it seems a little nickel-and-dimey to me. You pay per device, per user and per version. But it's incredibly highly rated and definitely one of the leaders.

- **Dashlane**
  dashlane.com

  If I hadn't started off with LastPass, I would probably embrace Dashlane for my password management. There is a free version, but for $40 a year, you get all the benefits of LastPass' premium version. Dashlane has the bonus feature of letting you change a bunch of passwords automatically in case of a breach. (LastPass makes it fairly easy now, but you still have to change them one by one.)

- **Keeper**
  keepersecurity.com

  NerdHerder Nancy Grubb says Keeper is a password manager and digital vault worth mentioning. "I like the security it seems to provide me for storing all my passwords in one place with one login," Nancy says.

- **RoboForm**
  roboform.com
  Another NerdHerder, Joanne St-Pierre from Niagara Falls Tourism, loves RoboForm for password management "because it remembers for me."

Three Non-Tech Password Management Techniques

1. **Make Up a Phrase**

   Come up with a fun, memorable phrase for each site. For LinkedIn, you might choose, "I am so glad Nerds are popular in 2015!" Then you'd take that phrase and use the first letter from each word. So your password might be *IasgNapi2015!*. The trick is that you'll still need to have a unique password for every site, so this could tax your memory. It would mine.

2. **Sandwich the Site**

   This method sounds easier: Bury the name of the site in a familiar phrase. For example I might choose, "I_love_Nerds_2015" as my phrase. Then my LinkedIn password might be *I_love_LinkedIn_Nerds_2015* and Facebook would be *I_love_Facebook_Nerds_2015*.

3. Carry a Card

The next step up from sticky notes is an innovative little site called PasswordCard (passwordcard.org). You generate a unique and complicated wallet-sized card that helps you choose random passwords for all your sites. PasswordCard also has an app to let you carry your card with you electronically.

Four Personal Finance Tools

Password thieves frequently go where the money is. These financial tools help you keep track of your finances and monitor your accounts for fraudulent activity.

1. Mint
mint.com

Mint, I tell you, Mint, Mint, Mint. This personal finance budget and money manager is always at the top of any list of best money tools. If you're new to money management tools, start here. Just ask everybody.

2. Moven
moven.com

For real-time budget management, you might try Moven. I'm not financially knowledgeable enough to figure out if Moven is a bank or a pre-paid debit card or some other kind of money pile, but the concept is this: You have money in an account with Moven (no fees). You can pay for things via a debit card and an app. When you buy something, Moven analyzes whether you're spending more than usual and how you spend your money.

3. **You Need a Budget**
   youneedabudget.com

   You guys know how much I love free stuff, so it's a little painful
   to recommend something that's $60 a year. But that's just $5 a
   month, and there are no other charges. People adore YNAB
   (that's what the cool kids call it) for personal budgeting,
   although there's much discussion about whether it can replace
   your business bookkeeping.

4. **Credit Karma**
   creditkarma.com

   We all should be incredibly paranoid about credit monitoring
   sites. Many of them require a credit card for "free monitoring,"
   and then the site charges your card every month even though
   you stopped monitoring your numbers, like a gym membership
   you never use. It took me a while to believe that Credit Karma
   was really not going to start draining my credit card with
   monthly charges once I signed up. But it kept its word, and I
   now keep track of my actual credit score with no strings
   attached. Yea for Credit Karma, and incredibly convenient and
   easy for me.

Collaborate

. . . .

In This Chapter:

PLUS

Trello

The project management world is a crowded space, but a few companies stand out. **Trello** offers an interesting take on project management by organizing your projects into "cards" that lay out like a deck across your screen. You can click on any card to flip it over and see the details, including tasks, collaborators and due dates.

Trello organizes all your projects into boards. Your account lets you have as many boards as you want, and you can manage the permissions for each for everything from read-only access to full privileges. You create lists and deadlines for each board, and you can assign tasks to others. It's easy to reprioritize and assign list items with a quick click and drag.

Trello Boards

Trello gets bonus points because it has personality. Several Trello rivals, such as Basecamp and Asana (Page 48), are pretty serious-looking tools: You can tell that they mean business. But Trello has a sense of playfulness as well as serious business features. You can choose bright, fun backgrounds for your projects, and a "Power-Up" feature (that doesn't even cost more money) lets your older cards show their age. (Gotta love the Pirate View.)

Collaborate

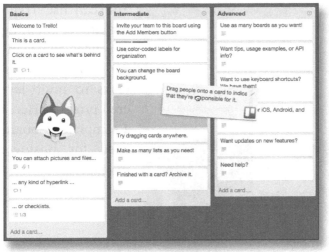

Trello Task Dragging

Beyond the cool dragging/dropping capability, you can create intricate lists and details on each card, which flips up when you click on it.

Trello Card Detail

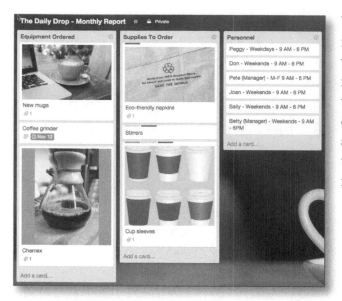

You can use Trello for almost anything you need to organize, from personal tasks to multi-layered projects. Here's a sample of a board used for business management.

Trello Business Management

In this sample, Trello tracks the sales opportunities for a real estate business.

Trello Sales Management

I've probably included enough examples, but here's an example of product development with the cutest task lists ever. "Cat Blocker"? Too funny.

Trello Project Management

4 Things to Know About Trello

1. Trello is a versatile task/project management tool that lets you organize your personal and business lives. The free version is robust for most small offices or solo businesses, and Trello Gold is a good bargain if you need more features.

2. Like many companies in this space, you can use Trello almost anywhere you hang out: online, with mobile apps, via email and more.

3. You can create as much detail as you need by creating individual boards then cards within boards then details on cards within boards.

4. Trello lets you collaborate with teams, assign tasks to yourself and others and set deadlines. Trello helps you keep up with the big picture with a dashboard, universal calendar, notifications and indicators that show forgotten projects.

Trello Alternatives

- **Basecamp**
  basecamp.com

  In 2004, a company called 37signals started creating online project management systems, primarily for the web design industry. Basecamp has evolved to be one of the most popular web-based project collaboration tools to share files, meet deadlines, assign tasks, centralize feedback and finish what you start.

  Basecamp is one of the most integrated project management services with a whole host of other integrations, including social networks, mobile phones and invoicing software. All the systems update each other and keep everyone on track. The company has changed its pricing structure multiple times since I started using it, and these days it's quite compatible with a small IT budget. One seriously cool benefit of Basecamp is that it's completely free for teachers, as long as they restrict their use to classroom work.

- **Asana**
  asana.com

  Another company-wide alternative to Trello is Asana. Asana is a tech blogger darling, and many organizations use it to coordinate projects and tasks.

- **Podio**
  podio.com

  Podio has the most flexibility when it comes to personalizing a tool to organize your business, but I find it to be the most complicated. You can add all kinds of things, such as events, inventory and projects. I find the set-up process confusing, and every time I've gone to create a project, I give up and just use something else. If you have the patience, it's a very powerful business and project management tool.

- **Smartsheet**
  smartsheet.com

  NerdHerder Chris Champion from the Institute of Public Works Engineering Australasia swears by this online collaborative spreadsheet. Chris says the hundreds of templates help him and his staff find just the right structure for any project they need to track.

NerdHerd Thumbs Up:
Basecamp juggles multiple projects

Lissa Clayborn from the Computer Science Teachers Association says she uses Basecamp to manage projects with multiple deadlines, tasks and project managers.

NerdHerd Thumbs Up: OfficeTime manages time, projects and finances

NerdHerder Celene Peurye from Focused Philanthropy uses the iOS product OfficeTime (officetime.net) for project management, but it also serves as her financial management system. OfficeTime lets her track her time, expenses and invoices in the same place.

Two Task List Tools

1. **Wunderlist**
   wunderlist.com

   Wunderlist is one of the most widely used task lists; and after receiving a whole bunch of investor money in 2013, it's poised to get even bigger. You can create and share lists, add things from anywhere, categorize with tags, set reminders and establish due dates. Of course, those features can be said of (almost?) all of the top task-list tools, but Wunderlist continues to expand in features and popularity. Since it integrated with Dropbox in the fall of 2014, you can expect more cross-platform connections with other major tools such as Evernote and Google tools.

   NerdHerders Gary Rifkin and Missy Malechek both give Wunderlist a thumbs up. Gary uses it to keep his teams informed and accountable, and Missy says, "Wunderlist helps me remember things where and when I need to remember them."

2. Todoist
todoist.com

Molly Gardner, one of our team members here at Your Nerdy Best Friend, swears her life was changed with Todoist. It shares many of the characteristics of Wunderlist (they're so similar that it amused me, and I had to put their feature lists side by side in the chart below.

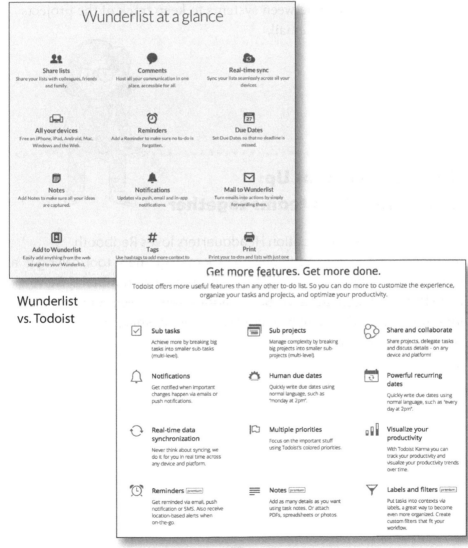

Wunderlist
vs. Todoist

Molly loves how Todoist helps keep the overwhelmed feeling at bay with a day or week view rather than a big old pile of undone stuff.

One of my favorite Todoist features is the capability to use plug-ins to turn emails into tasks. For example, a Chrome browser plug-in for Gmail will let me add an email as a task and assign it to someone else (passing the buck is my favorite pastime). This keeps Molly and me from having to switch back and forth between systems to keep track of the projects that come in via email.

NerdHerd Thumbs Up:
Redbooth brings teams together

Amy Williams from Association Headquarters loves Redbooth (redbooth.com), a collaboration and task management tool, calling it "a great project management tool for teams that work remotely." We've used Redbooth here at Nerdy BFF Headquarters as well, and the integration with Gmail made it our favorite for a while. Prices start at $5 per user per month.

ScheduleOnce

scheduleonce.com

How many emails does it take to set up a committee meeting? Let's see . . . you send one email to five people. Three people write you back with potential times. You write them back to thank them. Then you aggregate the options and email the group again. Then two people write that they can't make any of those times, and then you have to write back with new options (plus thank the two who wrote) . . . and on and on.

There has to be a better way.

ScheduleOnce is my favorite meeting scheduling tool. The site couples the high-tech interface with easy-to-understand functionality.

Unlike another popular scheduler, **Doodle** (Page 55), where you have to choose certain times and ask participants to pick, ScheduleOnce lets participants drag their mice over available blocks so the system can identify a common time when all participants can meet.

ScheduleOnce Schedule Management Page

Starting at $5 per month, ScheduleOnce also has capabilities to allow clients to pick their own appointment times. You can set up as many rules as you like to govern how people can set up appointments, such as the length of appointments and how much time you need between them.

ScheduleOnce offers convenient integrations to keep your schedule straight, including Google Calendar (Page 225) and Microsoft Outlook (Page 215). You can also hook up online meeting services such as GoToMeeting and WebEx (Page 73) to schedule online demos, and a widget can help your visitors schedule appointments straight from your site.

Nerd Know-How: Connect With Your Contacts

In theory, the ability to let customers set their own appointments sounds wonderful. The contacts can consult their schedules and choose the best time without going back and forth with you. But recently I encountered an automated system that left me feeling quite alienated. When I was trying to connect with a potential virtual assistant, she asked me to first fill out a form. Then she sent me an email to pick out a time for a consultation. The first appointments in her ScheduleOnce system were three weeks out. I was left feeling like she didn't want my business very much, and I stopped trying to connect. The lesson I learned: Even if it's inconvenient for you to stop and schedule an appointment, sometimes a personal touch goes a lot further than an automated system.

3 Things to Know About ScheduleOnce

1. ScheduleOnce is a scheduling system that helps you set up meetings without dozens of back-and-forth emails.

2. You have to register for an account to set up meetings, but people you invite don't have to.

3. Extra services that start at $5 a month let people schedule their own appointments on your calendar.

ScheduleOnce Alternatives

- **Doodle**
  doodle.com

  The first time I found Doodle, I sighed with happiness. Without ever entering your email address or any personal information, you can propose several dates and times for a meeting. Then Doodle generates a link for both your admin view and the participants' responses. You send the link to your participants, and everyone responds with availability, allowing you to use the admin view to find the perfect time.

	12:00 PM	3:00 PM	2:00 PM	9:00 AM
Sheldon Cooper		OK		OK
Leonard Hofstadter	OK		OK	
Rajesh Koothrappali	OK		OK	
Howard Wolowitz	OK		OK	
Count	3	1	3	1

Doodle Meeting Results Summary

I have used it for years, but recently it's upped its game to make it even more valuable. Now you can use the iOS or Android app to check on your schedules and propose more meetings. Plus it's added a service called a **MeetMe** page that gives you a private URL you can send to colleagues to let them propose a time to meet based on your availability. For the advanced features, you need to register for a free account and connect your calendar. Premium Doodle (That sounds funny, doesn't it?) starts at $39 a year.

Nerd Know-How: ScheduleOnce vs. Doodle

Although I like the functionality and look of ScheduleOnce more than Doodle, both have their uses. ScheduleOnce is great when you have a lot of flexibility in your schedule, but if you're just choosing among a few set times, Doodle is fast and easy. It's worth noting, though, that ScheduleOnce has a more professional look than Doodle.

- **WhenIsGood**
  whenisgood.net

  I used to use WhenIsGood, which is very easy and very cool but not very attractive. The main advantage over ScheduleOnce is that you don't have to register. Plus it has a free self-scheduling site, **youcanbook.me**, which integrates into your Google Calendar (Page 225).

Mon	Tue	Wed	Thu
21	**22**	**23**	**24**
Jul	Jul	Jul	Jul
10am	10am	10am	10am
15	15	15	15
30	30	30	30
45	45	45	45
11am	11am	11am	11am
15	15	15	15
30	30	30	30
45	45	45	45
12pm	12pm	12pm	12pm
15	15	15	15
30	30	30	30
45	45	45	45
1pm	1pm	1pm	1pm
15	15	15	15
30	30	30	30
45	45	45	45
2pm	2pm	2pm	2pm
15	15	15	15
30	30	30	30
45	45	45	45

WhenIsGood
Time Selection

- **TimeTrade**
  timetrade.com

  NerdHerder Mary Byers uses TimeTrade to let others schedule meetings with her. "It has saved me tons of time sending scheduling emails. I couldn't live without it now!"

- **Calendly**
  calendly.com

  I don't use this tool, but I had to include it after passionate praise from Stewart Rogers, the most famous "marketing technologist" and speaker/author I know (He's @TheRealSJR on Twitter). In Stewart's own words...

  > *After trying literally (not figuratively) every calendar booking and scheduling system available—including shared calendars like **Meetifyr**, **Meet-O-Matic** and Doodle (Page 55), busy-time sharing systems like ScheduleOnce (Page 53) and **TimeBridge**, and online booking systems like **Bookeo** and*

Meetin.gs—I finally found "the one"—and its name is Calendly. I even had an artificially intelligent assistant help me book meetings a few years ago (that solution has since been discontinued).

With Calendly, I am able to setup different meeting types, such as a 15-minute call, a "conference get-together" and a 60-minute physical meeting. I only have to do this once when I'm setting up the system to meet my needs. Each of these meeting types receives its own URL, and each can have its own rules, descriptions and instructions. I can say how many of those types of meeting I want to have in 24 hours, how much notice needs to be given, what buffer time I want before and after, which days and times I want to make available and more.

If you want to book a call or meeting with me, I simply send you the appropriate URL (or the main URL—you then get to pick the meeting type), and you see a beautifully designed, responsive website that shows my available time slots. Calendly syncs with my Google Calendar (Page 225), so you'll only see truly available slots. You pick a slot, and a short form at the end tells me how to contact you on the day. Whatever you pick goes directly into both our calendars.

The whole system is slick, quick, and beautifully simple. Calendly lets me outsource my schedule to the people that want to speak with me, and automates the booking process. No more "calendar tennis."

NerdHerd Thumbs Up: Doodle makes meetings easy

Doodle is a favorite tool for scheduling meetings for both Anne Lupkoski and Roberta Scarrow. Anne says, "Doodle makes it easy to reach and hear back from multiple people and to see their availability."

Three Tools to Manage Your Relationships

Once you figure out how to meet with your contacts, you need to organize them. Choosing a customer relationship management tool is quite complicated. Here at Nerdy HQ, we still struggle with finding the right set of features that will help us keep track of conversations, follow up with inquiries, manage the logistics process and basically keep our heads on straight. Like many of the tools in this book, CRM solutions are insanely varied and numerous. The options below represent some broad strokes of the types of CRMs that should serve as a starting point for your search.

1. **Salesforce**
   salesforce.com

   You might call Salesforce the grandfather of the cloud-based CRM systems. In fact, it's one of the pioneers in the software-as-a-service (SaaS) space, which transformed much of the technology we use from downloadable programs that worked on one machine at a time to cloud-based systems that synchronized data among a multitude of users and devices.

Nerd Know-How:
Save Money on Salesforce

If you don't need to manage contracts and projects through Salesforce, you can choose the Contact Manager Edition, which is just $5 per user per month. Our office found this to be a great solution for tracking conversations and leads to keep us all on the same page.

The kicker is that the Contact Manager Edition is really hard to find on its site since Salesforce would much rather you sign up for the $25+ level. Use this link to get started with the Contact Manager Edition:

salesforce.com/form/contact/contact-manager.jsp

Salesforce's main services start at $25 per user per month. This will get you the ability to manage an unlimited number of contacts, plus create and track contracts, proposals, projects and more. Salesforce also integrates with a myriad of other apps to facilitate everything from accounting to interoffice chat to email. The system is entirely customizable for any number of business models. It's a great place to start your research.

2. **Contactually**
   contactually.com

Contactually comes highly recommended by many of my friends in the speaker business. The system helps you and your team members remember to reach out, follow up and stay in touch with your contacts.

You organize your contacts into "buckets," and you may have too much fun playing the Bucket Game. Your contacts appear above all your little buckets (which look like buckets), and you have to sort before the time runs out. The video-game challenge helps you race through the sorting of hundreds of contacts.

Contactually also helps you connect with your contacts in the social media world, giving you insight like Discover.ly (Page 208). The system is a little pricy, at least for a small office like ours: It starts at $29 per user per month.

3. **Nimble**
   nimble.com

   Nimble's premise is that connections should be made everywhere your contacts hang out. Nimble is particularly feature-rich when it comes to social media. The system puts all your social media feeds into one place so you can engage with your leads and prospects as they move around the web. That last statement may make the tool sound a little stalker-ish, but the format is just proof that this is a true tool for our social-network connected times.

   Nimble has a simple pricing structure: $15 per user per month. NerdHerder Beth Bridges, aka The Networking Motivator, says Nimble "is powerful and easy to use, and it unifies my contacts and social media to help me stay connected to my network."

Nerd Know-How:
A Little Stalking Is OK

I'm keeping my eye on a little tech tool called Charlie (charlieapp.com), which scans your upcoming meetings and sends you a one-page briefing on your attendees. CEO Aaron Frazin caught my attention when he sent me an email detailing what Charlie had found out about me.

Charlie's research found that:

- *You just reached your fundraising goal on Kickstarter for **"27+ Best Apps for Work."** Congrats!*

- *You love **Travel** and **Marathons***

- *You were a **Peace Corps** volunteer*

- *I hear you can make some mean **McDonald's** French fries. Can I try some?*

I asked Aaron how his tool differed from Discoverly (Page 208) and Tempo (Page 229), and he said, "Our whole goal is to be your executive assistant and do the deep dive for you so you don't really need to do much reading. We watched hundreds of executive assistants prepare for their meetings and we've automated that process. So not only do we send you intel about the person you meet with, but also we'll deep dive into their company and even take away articles that we don't think you'll want to read."

The app is still a little quirky, but we're optimistic that it'll be helpful.

Join.me

Join.me is the answer to the question, "Why don't I just show you what I mean?" when you're on the phone with a colleague. You can either download its teeny-tiny app onto your desktop and start a meeting anytime, or visit the site and let the prompts guide you.

The pro versions start at $15 a month, but the free version is perfect for those quick collaborations to walk up to 10 people through something you're seeing on your screen. Even in the free version, you can share files, let someone else take over controls and route your conversation through the computer rather than a phone line.

Its mobile apps let you join a session on the go, and the pro versions let you initiate a meeting via iPad.

Nerd Know-How:
Solve Emergencies from Anywhere

Join.me is absolutely wonderful for office emergencies. Once I was in line to board a four-hour flight, and my assistant was desperately trying to get a file ready for a client. He was having trouble, and I was able to see his screen on my phone with Join.me and help him find what we needed before I boarded the plane. Emergency solved!

Start a Join.me Meeting

The start menu from the app makes it pretty clear what you can do.

1. To start a meeting, the free version gives you a one-time code. If you pay for the service, you can claim a custom URL.

2. If you're joining a session, just enter the code provided by the meeting organizer.

Join.me Start Menu

Once you start a session, you can (from left to right) start an online call, chat with participants, start/stop showing your screen and see who joined. When you click on the participants, you can also share files and pass the control of your computer to someone else. (I did this with my mother once to show her where her photos were stored. She called me a hacker.) The last button shows several premium options, such as scheduling and recording an event.

Join.me Action Menu

The other attendees will see your screen along with their own little control menu. Here's a screenshot of what I saw via the web browser when I joined my own session while writing this. It's a sad day when a nerd joins her own meeting just to have company.

Join.me Participant View

NerdHerd Thumbs Up:
Join.me facilitates collaboration

NerdHerder Kathy Benton loves Join.me because it easily shares screens for presentations and collaboration.

4 Things to Know About Join.me

1. Join.me is an instant screensharing tool for when you need to literally be on the same page with someone from afar.

2. The free version is perfect for small meetings of 10 people or fewer. Starting at $15 a month, you can invite up to 250 people, which puts it into webinar territory.

3. It's pretty persistent in asking you to upgrade, but I don't blame the company for wanting to make a buck, you know.

4. As with all online meetings, the quality of everyone's Internet connection is a major issue. You increase frustration instead of efficiency if your connection is slow and everyone sees your screen a few beats behind.

Nerd Know-How:
Access Your Computer Remotely

In 2014 Google Chrome added a remote access tool called, interestingly enough, **Google Remote**. Once you enable the plug-in and set up an access code, you can access your computer from other computers. (You'll also need Google Remote on the remote computer.) You can also give others access to your machine.

Zoom

If everyone in your online meeting promises to wear pants, videoconferencing can be a great way to communicate. You'll find a lot of common features among the videoconferencing and screensharing tools, but **Zoom** is stepping up and standing out.

Videoconferencing

Zoom will blow you away with the ease of starting a videoconference. From any computer or iOS/Android device, a quick download lets you start a meeting. With a couple of clicks, you can see your own video image on your screen and invite others. The video quality is super duper, and the audio is great as well.

In a meeting, you can collaborate and share in a number of ways.

From a Mac or PC:

- View everyone in a meeting on one screen. Zoom can automatically change the spotlight to the person who is speaking.

- Share your screen and give control to other attendees (even in the free version).

- Choose which window to share, or share your whole desktop. If you have two monitors, you can show one desktop or the other.

Zoom Collaboration

1. A menu bar gives you sharing options, audio/video control, participant management and annotation functions.

2. When you are viewing a shared screen, the participants will shrink to smaller windows so you can still interact.

Zoom Collaboration

3. You can allow participants to annotate your screen with arrows, lines and more.

Sharing Mobile Screens

When you start or join a Zoom meeting from a mobile device, you can share photos, go to a web page or share files from a number of cloud services.

Zoom Mobile Share Options

Once you share something, you and your colleagues can use tools to highlight and annotate as you discuss.

Mobile Annotation Options

Bonus Awesomeness

One of the coolest Zoom features is the ability to share your iOS device via your computer.

When you choose to share your iPhone/iPad, Zoom lets you create a link to an iOS device on the same Wi-Fi connection via AirPlay. A dialog box gives you step-by-step instructions to mirror the screen of your iOS device to your computer so attendees can see apps and activities on your device.

Zoom Sharing Options for Computers

Cool, eh?

Nerd Know-How: Record Demos of Your Devices

I'm not advocating zooming with yourself, but some of the features of Zoom are useful for more than collaborating. Since the free version of Zoom lets you record your presentation, you can start a screensharing session and capture a demo with voiceover on your computer. And since Zoom lets you share your mobile device, you can even do a demo of an app on your tablet or phone.

Don't have Zoom? Another secret weapon for creating a mobile demo is the **Reflector App** (airsquirrels.com/reflector) in conjunction with Jing (Page 78). Reflector lets you show your mobile screen on your computer, and Jing lets you capture a picture or video with voiceover.

NerdHerd Thumbs Up: Zoom brings teams together

Debbie Lowenthal from Association Resources likes the option of video for her team's virtual conferences. Kerri Wilson says Zoom "saves windshield time" and is convenient and easy to use.

4 Things to Know About Zoom

1. Zoom is a videoconferencing tool with screensharing and recording features.

2. Up to 25 people can conference in via audio and/or video from any device. With a paid version, you can have up to 100 people.

3. Zoom lets you share your mobile devices through your laptop, which means you can demo an app on your phone to members of the meeting.

4. Zoom lets you have a one-to-one connection for as long as you want for free, but additional connections require a subscription if you're going to meet for more than 40 minutes.

Alternatives to Join.me and Zoom

Whew—this is has become a crowded market. I rely on Join.me because parent company LogMeIn has proved itself incredibly reliable. And Zoom is fairly new but seems to be unbreakable. But I could have easily chosen any of these other solid tools in the online meeting department:

- **Google Hangouts**
  google.com/hangouts

  Google Hangouts lets up to 10 people connect via video. You can share your screens, include professional-looking name banners across the bottom of the screen and even wear virtual tiaras and fake mustaches during your chats.

  Google Hangouts can also be used for a bigger audience with its Hangouts On Air feature. This allows you to broadcast your Hangout live to YouTube (Page 72), and afterward your presentation is instantly archived.

Nerd Know-How:
Make the Most of Google+ Hangouts

I'm completely enamored with the concept of Google Hangouts, but in practice, I've heard several stories of people giving up on the service because of jerky video and other challenges. Google doesn't tolerate mediocrity very well, so I'm guessing it'll make it awesome or make it disappear. But that doesn't mean that others don't swear by it, like fellow nerd (and brilliant dude) Terry Brock (terrybrock.com).

> *For me, using Google+ Hangouts is a fabulous resource. I can reach hundreds of thousands, even millions, over YouTube and get a message out for clients. I use this as a part of my speaking, regularly offering a Google+ Hangout before an event to help set the stage before speaking. It provides a way to connect with people, get their feedback and make the connection more human. The fact that it also records the event and makes it available on demand on YouTube is ideal. I highly recommend using this tool.*

- **AnyMeeting**
  anymeeting.com

Before Zoom came along, my favorite free webinar tool was AnyMeeting, which lets you share your screen with up to 25 people for free. It used to let you record the sessions on the free plan, but now you'll have to pay $18 a month. But if you sell tickets to your event (integrated into the registration system), AnyMeeting takes a small portion and upgrades you to the ad-free version. And AnyMeeting lets you hold a videoconference with up to six participants for free.

AnyMeeting is also a great choice if your presentation includes video because it allows you to play a YouTube video (Page 218) that runs locally on each attendee's connection rather than through the streaming presentation (which can make it look like a French Impressionist painting).

- **Skype**
  skype.com

  An oldie but an increasingly valuable goodie, Skype is making a comeback. In 2014 Skype introduced real-time translation services. That means you can speak English to someone who speaks only Spanish, and the system will translate you. Crazy, huh? (Also see Google Translate, Page 237.)

  Skype has also integrated its chat services with Microsoft Office, plus it has dropped the premium version and now gives all kinds of bonus features away. Jocelyn Boland, a NerdHerder from Southeastern Insurance Consultants, recommends Skype as a great way to keep up with family and friends.

- **WebEx** and **GoToMeeting**
  webex.com and **gotomeeting.com**

  These two providers represent the state-of-the-art technology (and pricing) in the online meeting arena. For smaller organizations, the pricing can be prohibitive, especially if you don't do many online meetings or events. But both services offer free versions that let up to three people meet and share info.

- **UberConference** and **Speek**
  uberconference.com and **speek.com**

  Who'da thunk that technology startups would seek to make teleconferencing more fun? The new options for meeting with people via phone are very cool, indeed. Instead of using the traditional phone number and PIN code, the new systems from companies such as UberConference and Speek connect with the web, smart devices and your computer with just a click of a button rather than a series of pound signs and access codes.

Both systems show participants on a dashboard, and they'll even dial participants rather than making them dial in. They both have free versions and monthly plans (less than $20 a month). Speek offers some screensharing capabilities and is a little more expensive.

Four Tools to Check Your Internet Strength

No matter which wonderful online conferencing service you choose, everything is going to suck if your Internet is slow. These sites test the strength of your connections so you can use the best form of communication for online meetings.

1. **Hotel WiFi Test**
   hotelwifitest.com

   You don't have to wait until you're in the hotel robe before checking the Wi-Fi strength. The Hotel WiFi Test reports the signal strength from hotels around the world. When you're shopping for the perfect place to check the office email in between trips to the pool, you can look up hotels and check their Wi-Fi ratings before you choose.

2. **Down for Everyone or Just Me?**
   downforeveryoneorjustme.com

   Have you ever been surfing the web and come across a down page? Maybe I'm a little paranoid, but my first thought is always, "I wonder if this is down for everyone or just me?"

Guess what? There's a site for that. Just type the URL in question into the perfectly named site downforeveryoneorjustme.com. The service checks the offending site to see if it's an isolated problem.

3. **Speedtest.net** and 4. **Pingtest.net**

Most of us depend on a strong Internet connection to make sure we can upload, download and access what we need from the web and the cloud. These two sites run tests on your connection to make sure you're fast enough to do what you need to do. I've used them to prove to my provider that my connection wasn't as fast as it should be; and when I travel, I check a connection before choosing between my personal hotspot or the hotel's.

NerdHerd Thumbs Up: Padlet facilitates togetherness

Padlet (padlet.com) promotes itself as "possibly the easiest way to create and collaborate in the world," and that may be true. Click the "Create Something" button, and you get an empty page that acts as a bulletin board for file sharing or any kind of information. NerdHerder Diane Hanel recommends it. "When I am promoting an event or topic, I can have all of the information available on a website."

Nerd Know-How: Be a Wi-Fi-Savvy Traveler

Most travelers are light users of hotel Wi-Fi services. They write a few emails, post an update on Facebook and perhaps surf the web awhile. But if you're doing some serious work in a hotel, be aware that your connection may be both unsecure and unstable. On the rare occasion when I have to present a webinar from a hotel, I will call multiple times to verify its Wi-Fi capabilities. Almost without fail, the reality does not live up to the promises. And if you try to use your own hotspot to connect, the hotel may block the signal so you have to pay for its slower systems.

Things may improve. In 2014, the Marriott hotel chain paid a $600,000 fine for blocking personal hotspots at its Gaylord Opryland hotel in Nashville. The Federal Communications Commission seems to be trending toward protecting existing Wi-Fi from "willful interference."

Bonus Utility:
SupportDetails.com
Do you draw a blank when an IT troubleshooter asks you what version of operating system you're on? Visit this site from any browser (mobile or desktop), and all your specs will magically appear.

Share

In This Chapter:

PLUS

Jing

techsmith.com/jing

Every once in a while, you need to capture a picture or video of what you're seeing on a screen. One of my favorite free tools of all time is **Jing,** a download from TechSmith (techsmith.com) that makes the screencapture process insanely easy. Jing is one of those tools that you'll reach for multiple times a week as you find more and more ways to use it.

NerdHerd Thumbs Up: The many applications of Jing and Snagit

I've been sharing Jing and Snagit (Jing's big brother, Page 80) at my sessions for several years, and many readers have found all kinds of ways to use them. Logan Beszterda from Association Management Consultants, LLC, loves Jing for creating how-to videos and graphics. American Mensa's Pam Donahoo says, "It's so great that I can point my team members to exactly what I am seeing and thinking. Despite all my efforts, they can't always read my mind." And Kimberly Lilley uses Jing for expense reports to capture an image of every payment and add notes.

Snagit is a "snipping tool on steroids," says one NerdHerder. Shawn Powelson says Snagit makes it easy to proof advertisements, communicate exactly what you're seeing and use text and arrows and more to explain and describe.

Seven Ways to Use Jing

1. Give feedback on a document or web page.

2. Point out a typo on a website.

3. Draw a map.

4. Grab an ungrab-able graphic from the web (not in a copyright-infringement way, of course).

5. Make a quick video to remind yourself how you figured out that one report you have to run every year.

6. Create a series of training videos for employees or volunteers.

7. Show your IT department that weird thing that keeps happening on your computer.

Screencaptures with Jing

Jing sits on the edge of your screen in the form of a little yellow sun, which you can move around your monitor.

Jing on the Screen

When you scroll over the sun, three buttons pop out. The crosshairs button gives you the ability to highlight a portion of the screen. You can also use computer shortcuts to start a capture without clicking the button. Once you have your screen highlighted, you can choose to capture a picture of the screen to annotate (a screenshot) or start a movie that captures your voice and every movement on the screen (a screencast).

Jing Screenshot Dialog Box

Screenshot Options

1. The screenshot tool has a variety of features for annotation. You can add an arrow, a text box, a highlight box and text highlights.

2. Once you use one of the tools, you can modify styles such as colors and fonts.

3. Jing can save and share your screencaptures in a variety of ways, including a one-click connection to an online media-hosting site called **Screencast.com** (also free from TechSmith). You can also save the capture or copy to paste into an email or file.

4. If you own Jing's big brother, **Snagit** ($50), you can choose to edit your capture with Snagit's advanced editing tools such as borders and stamps and a blur tool to obscure private information. You can also capture scrolling screens with Snagit. I used Snagit to capture and annotate the examples for this book.

Nerd Know-How: Share Jing Graphics

When you share the link that Screencast.com automatically generates, it goes to a separate page. If you're sharing on social media, go to the Screencast.com page and right click on your image to get the URL of the image itself rather than the hosting page. That way your graphic shows up directly in the post.

Screencast Options

One of the most helpful features of Jing is its ability to capture your voice and computer actions with just a couple of clicks.

When you click the video capture button, you can choose to mute the microphone or do a voiceover. The app gives you a count-down before the recording starts. Jing lets you make a video of up to 5 minutes, but you can pause the recording if you're switching screens or prepping something else you want to demo.

Jing Video Capture Button

Jing Video Capture Dialog Box

4 Things to Know About Jing

1. Jing is a free download for Macs and PCs that lets you capture, annotate and animate what you're seeing on your screen.

2. Jing is integrated with Screencast.com, which allows you to send your screencaptures (both videos and images) to the web with just a click. Jing will give you an instant web address to share, and the recipients can see your content without downloading Jing or special software. You can also save or copy Jing content.

3. Once you discover Jing, you will figure out dozens of ways you can use it to save time and eliminate confusion.

4. Jing doesn't have a pro version, but you can purchase TechSmith's Snagit for about $50 for advanced features such as one-click uploads to YouTube and extensive editing tools. The next level up for screencaptures with TechSmith is **Camtasia**, which starts at about a hundred bucks. I own both Snagit and Camtasia, but for a quick capture, my favorite is always Jing.

Nerd Know-How: Solve Jing Temper Tantrums

Jing operates with Java plus its own software, and sometimes the program gets cranky. You may see an error when you try to play a screencast video if your Java plug-ins are out of date. If Jing starts giving you trouble, Google the error code or text, and you can generally find easy fixes.

NerdHerd Thumbs Up: M8 Apps keep information organized

As an admin, Kimberly Chatak-Nelson says she moves data all day long. The slightly quirky site named M8 (m8software.com) offers several Windows PC tools that help you organize information, clip more than one item at the same time and more. Kimberly says the free clipboard app helps her store and organize tons of text and graphic clips.

Jing Alternatives

- **FastStone Capture** (Windows)
  faststone.org

  FastStone Capture is a Windows app with a great reputation. You can capture windows, a full screen, a scrolling screen and a video with audio. In addition, when you capture something, you get a whole host of editing options to add a little more flair and details.

  FastStone has a couple of extra handy tools such as a screen magnifier plus a color picker. You have a number of ways to export your capture, but I still prefer Jing's integration with Screencast.com. But the FastStone touchscreen functionality for Windows 8 seems pretty darn cool. It has a free version as well as an upgrade for a one-time fee of $19.95.

- **QuickTime** (Mac)
  apple.com/quicktime

  Believe it or not, the free version of QuickTime on Macs includes screen recording. Sorry, PC folks—it's not available for Windows.

- **Screencast-O-Matic**
  screencast-o-matic.com

  If you need a capture tool that runs from a browser, just visit Screencast-o-matic.com and click the "Start Capture" button to instantly make recordings up to 15 minutes long. It runs on Java, which may be blocked at your work or worrisome to your IT department.

  The free version gives you all kinds of extras, such as including your webcam in the broadcast and animated mouse clicks. But if you don't pay the $15 a year (which includes even more extras), you have to live with the company's watermark.

Nerd Know-How:
Capture Screens on Windows

Glinda the Good Witch told Dorothy that the solution she sought was with her all along—such is the case for screenshots! The **Windows Snipping Tool** is built into Windows operating systems and lets you capture what you need on a screen with just a couple of clicks. Then you can annotate it and share, just like Jing.

So why use Jing? Well, it's just cuter.

Adobe Reader

get.adobe.com/reader

If you haven't taken a close look at your regular old **Adobe Reader**, you are missing out in a big way. Reader XI, released in the fall of 2012, contains capabilities that can change the way you work with PDFs—without downloading new software or paying the big bucks.

When you open Reader, check out the top right of the screen. You can add notes to documents, cross out and replace text, fill out forms, and track changes from multiple editors. You can even add audio notes and a stamp.

Adobe Reader Comment Menu

Signing Feature

The coolest feature of the new-generation Reader is the ability to sign a document. No more printing out a PDF, signing it, then scanning it back in and attaching it to an email. Now you can just load your signature into the program, then click and paste it where you want it.

Adobe Reader Sign Feature

To load your signature, you can upload a scan of your signature, sign on a track pad or use a built-in stylized signature in Reader.

1. Add text to fill out forms.
    Tip: If you have lots of form fields, it can be hard to line up all the text boxes and make it look neat. Try **FillAnyPDF.com** instead.

2. Quickly check a box in a form.

3. Place your signature or add initials with just a click.

4. If you want to track signatures, you can click the "Send or Collect Signatures" button, which takes you to the Adobe site to set up an EchoSign account.

5. You can place your signature and move it where you want it.

Nerd Know-How: Send a Signed PDF

Adobe Reader will really try hard to get you to send your document through Adobe's solution for signature tracking and more paid goodies. It's all tied in with the new Acrobat DC, Adobe's cloud service. You also have to register with Adobe to use it. If you don't need extensive tracking options, just ignore those pop-ups and buttons. Simply save the signed PDF as a separate file and send it as an attachment.

3 Things to Know About Adobe Reader XI

1. Adobe Reader is a tool we probably all have on our machines but don't use to its fullest capabilities. The best feature is that you can sign and annotate PDFs without any special software.

2. Unless you need signature tracking, skip the "Get Others to Sign" option and just save the signed PDF as a new file and send via email.

3. The mobile apps allow you to do everything on the go, including signing documents with your finger on touchscreens. In 2015 Adobe also added an app called Fill & Sign, which lets you, believe it or not, fill and sign PDF forms, plus an advanced Adobe Acrobat app. They're both tied with the Acrobat DC paid service.

Adobe Reader XI Alternatives

- **Nitro Reader**
  gonitro.com/pdf-reader

  For Windows machines, you can't beat the functionality of the free Nitro Reader, which lets you create PDFs as well as annotate and collaborate.

- **iAnnotate**
  branchfire.com/iannotate

  This mobile app, which is available for Android and iOS, gives you editing and reading tools for PDFs and more. It also integrates with popular cloud storage services such as Box, Dropbox and Google Drive (Page 8).

NerdHerd Thumbs Up: DocuSign and Sign Easy facilitate signing on the go

Two NerdHerders shared tools that help you easily keep track of everything you need to close a project. Wayne King from Coldwell Banker Residential Brokerage says DocuSign (docusign.com) helps manage electronic signatures for transaction documents. "It saves time, money and paper," Wayne says. "All copies are legible as they are all originals."

Thom Singer, the genius behind the Cool Things Entrepreneurs Do podcast, uses Sign Easy (getsigneasy.com) to sign contracts and other PDFs on mobile devices. Thom says Sign Easy "makes me more productive when I'm away from my computer."

Three Green Tools

You can run a more environmentally sensitive office by not printing out your PDFs or use any one of these paper-saving tools.

1. **PaperKarma**
   paperkarma.com

   If you're not careful, mail-order catalogs can take over your kitchen table. Reclaim your space and get rid of the waste with PaperKarma, an easy-to-use tool that helps you unsubscribe from mailing lists with a couple of clicks on your phone.

   You simply take a picture of the address label with the scanning codes and submit it to PaperKarma. It contacts the sender for you and request that you be removed from the list. The app tracks your submissions and lets you know when you've been removed—all without any work from you.

PaperKarma had an identity crisis for a while when it was purchased by Reputation.com. It tried to charge for the service after a certain number of requests, but I think it's 100 percent free again.

2. Print Friendly and **3. The Printliminator**
printfriendly.com and
css-tricks.com/examples/ThePrintliminator

Print Friendly takes any web page and reformats it for printing, making sure you don't waste pages when the text runs off the page. You can also easily remove pictures for printing or save as a PDF. The Printliminator does the same thing with a little bookmarklet in your bookmarks bar.

NerdHerd Thumbs Up: SkyView app puts things in perspective

My best friend from college, NerdHerder Roki VW, is a physician with a really tough specialty. She uses the SkyView app to step outside and clear her brain by looking through the phone viewfinder at the sky. "It's a nice way to break from the stressful work that happens at night… step out into the cool air and go someplace else in my mind."

Issuu

• •

Have you ever created a fantastic PDF brochure or report and invited people to download it—where it promptly dissolved from a well-designed piece to a string of boring pages that scroll one after another after another?

The mystical, magical site called **Issuu** transforms your boring document into an interactive, dynamic, interesting online magazine, book or catalog that people can flip through. The graphics of the viewing interface will make you look like a pro, and it has built-in features that allow readers to share and download your files.

Transforming your boring document into an online magazine is embarrassingly simple. Just drag a file to the uploader, name your document, add a description and press a button. Issuu will process your file in no

Issuu Layout

time and then provide you with everything you need to share your new magazine.

1. Issuu lets you create booklets from any standard document format. The sample on the previous page is a yearbook I put together of tech tools from my newsletters in 2013 and 2014. The Issuu version creates a shadow that looks like a page division in a book. Users click to make the pages turn.

2. When you import a document, you can add hyperlinks or internal links for navigation within the document. Readers can scroll over a link to click through, share or comment.

Embed Issuu on Your Site

I like to embed the Issuu publications into my website to make it look like cool people work here. It's incredibly easy to create the code to embed it. You can choose the size, what page shows first, the color of the background and whether the page flips on its own.

Nerd Know-How:
Create Attention-Getting
Documents for a Web Page

Want your documents to stand out? Choose to Autoflip the pages so that your document animates by itself when visitors browse the page. You can also choose a two-page spread so people know it's a magazine.

Add it to your site

Open publication - Free publishing

▼ Styling options

Size [650] x [244] px

Page   Start on page [1 ⬍]

Layout   ☐ Autoflip the pages

Color [Orange ⬍] [#e67728]

Show   ☑ Social options menu (?)

Save style   ☐ Use on Tumblr or other blog (?)

Embed code <div data-configid="3562425/8738129" style="width: 525px; height: 197px;" class="issuuembed"></div><script type="text/javascript" src="//e.issuu.com/embed.js" async="true"></script>

Issuu Add to Site Menu

Issuu Statistics

One of the wonderful things about Issuu is the capability to see statistics about your publications. Issuu has a robust free version that gives you six months of statistics. Paid versions (starting at $29 a month) come without ads and give you more statistics.

Issuu Lifetime Statistics

The statistics get quite granular and can give you real insight into publication use and popularity. You can find out how many people saw your publication, how long they spent looking at it and even how much they hung out on one particular page.

Issuu Page Performance

Issuu looks great on mobile devices, and in 2014 it added another social feature that lets a reader clip a portion of the screen for commenting and sharing.

5 Things to Know About Issuu

1. Issuu lets you take almost any document and turn it into a flippable magazine.

2. You can embed Issuu into your website, share the link to the main site, distribute via social media and even order a (pretty pricy) hard copy straight from the site.

3. The free version of Issuu has ads for other publications, and you have no control over their content. FlipSnack (See alternatives, below) might be a better option if you have a school-age audience or want to limit the chance that ads that show up with your document will be off-topic or offensive.

4. Issuu has a hidden benefit—SEO. Google and other search engines will index your publications and give you added exposure on the web.

5. You can pay to promote your publications on the Issuu platform to increase readership. The advertising options let you choose a daily budget and fine-tune other settings.

Issuu Alternatives

- **FlipSnack**
  flipsnack.com and **flipsnackedu.com**

  FlipSnack has similar functionality but doesn't show ads. Its free version limits you to 15 pages and has other restrictions, but the paid versions start at just $12 a month. When you get to the $16 level, you get the full line of **SnackTools** (snacktools.com), which include website and banner designs, polls, and slideshows. The suite is pretty cool, so I'm not sure why SnackTools is not more popular.

- **FlippingBook Software**
  flippingbook.com

  I prefer the ease of an online site that does all the work for me, but you can also buy software to manage your own, especially if you are creating regular flip books. Check out the aptly named FlippingBook software starting at $399 or less expensive alternatives such as **A-PDF FlipBook Creator** (a-pdf.com/flipbook-creator) starting at $99.

- **Kindle Direct Publishing**
  kdp.amazon.com

  Kindle from Amazon.com is just one of the many places you can publish material for eReaders. You won't pay anything to upload and publish your book, but it has requirements about setting the prices of books that are a certain size. Another option is Apple **iBooks Author** (apple.com/ibooks-author).

- **CreateSpace**
  createspace.com

  If you really like the idea of creating your online book that flips, why not just create a real book that flips? Just take your print-ready book in PDF form and upload it, then add cover art and press publish. In just a few days, you can have a hard copy in your hands.

  This is a great option for publishing a cool internal book (such as a history of your organization or an office manual), or you can assemble the great American novel. Some people have created custom children's books for the kids in their families for very little money. CreateSpace is an Amazon company, so you can also publish it straight to the site or distribute it to other booksellers. Most of the features of the service are free, though you pay a little extra here and there for expanded distribution and a custom ISBN number.

Four Ways to Create
Your Own Content Libraries

Issuu is wonderful for organizing and curating your content. These tools go further by curating the news and updates you need to stay current and speak knowledgably at parties.

1. **Flipboard**
   flipboard.com

   Flipboard is a resource I use every single day. The content curating platform can import all your RSS feeds plus give you access to amazing, customized content—all in a clever, attractive magazine format. I created my own board called Nerdy News where I collect and share my favorite tech content with hundreds of followers. I flip through dozens of articles a day and save the ones I want. When it's time to blog or put together another NerdWords newsletter, I go back through my archives and find the best stuff I've saved.

   My friend and NerdHerder Kathryn Giblin is a very busy international consultant and trainer. She loves Flipboard because it brings together her news and information feeds and lets her access the information on the go.

2. **Feedly**
   feedly.com

   Feedly has been around a while, but it got a huge boost when Google Reader shut down in 2013.

3. **Pocket**
   getpocket.com

   Pocket allows you to tuck any article or website into a virtual folder to read later from anywhere: Nooks, Android devices, iOS devices, desktops and other devices. You'll find options to save to Pocket on many major sites and readers, allowing you to instantly add articles and pages to your account to read anywhere. A completely useable version of Pocket is free, but it does have a premium level as well.

4. **Evernote**
   evernote.com

   Evernote was made for creating libraries. Learn all about Evernote starting on Page 14.

NerdHerd Thumbs Up:
Next Issue brings you the
most-read magazines for ten bucks a month

NerdHerder Sharmaine Battaglia Hamilton likes to take a whole rack of magazines with her through her subscription to Next Issue (nextissue.com).

Prezi

prezi.com

● ●

For—I don't know, 200 years?—the standard for presentations has been Microsoft's **PowerPoint**. Ever since we dropped the overhead projector/transparency model, we've emphasized key points of our educational sessions with bullet-point slides.

Although PowerPoint is still the most popular program, it has become the software we love to hate. That's why we're always looking for alternatives; and in any conversation about the best ways to avoid PowerPoint, we must mention **Prezi**.

The concept of Prezi is completely innovative. Pretend you have a giant whiteboard with all your information for your presentation. As the presenter, you have a high-quality video camera. As you tell your story, you zoom in and out of relevant areas of the whiteboard, even rotating the camera into new areas to draw people's attention to the right elements.

● ●

NerdHerd Thumbs Up: Prezi creates engaging presentations

Ashley Kowal gives Prezi high ratings for livening up her programs. "I love creating engaging presentations that offer greater flexibility than PowerPoint."

● ●

Nerd Know-How:
Don't Make Audience Members Dizzy

To tell you the truth, I don't care for Prezi. A half a dozen times I've been determined to convert one of my programs into this nerd-friendly format with the "Oh . . . cool!" factor. I start designing away, but the learning curve seems to be higher than my patience level. And I find all that zooming in and out and the "camera moving" effects to be dizzying for me and for my attendees. That being said, others LOVE Prezi, like fellow speaker Roger Courville (thevirtualpresenter.com):

"Prezi's best when you understand how motion contributes to the communication. Animation can be great to communicate directionality or relationship or hierarchy, but skip the flying-things-from-Mars-to-get-attention stuff."

Create a Presentation with Prezi

1. As with PowerPoint, your content will be organized by slides even though the final Prezi looks nothing like a slide-based presentation. Each slide represents where your Prezi will move next. This slide shows an overview of the

Prezi Overview

whole presentation, as if the camera zoomed all the way out to show you the outline of your presentation.

2. You can change the way the Prezi moves from slide to slide with the Edit Path controls. On templates like this desktop theme, this means you can "fly your camera" from the plant to the bookshelf and back to the clock.

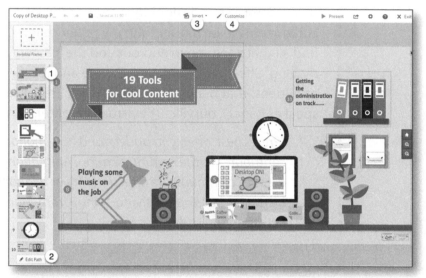

Prezi Edit Path View

3. You can insert a heck of a lot of cool things into Prezi, such as YouTube videos. (Make sure your Internet connection is strong so you can stream it without buffering.) You can also import a PowerPoint presentation into your Prezi, and the slides will import as separate Prezi slides. You'll have to work with the PowerPoint slides awhile to give them that Prezi look because they import in a pretty boring format stripped of any animations or fancy effects.

4. The Customize button gives you color schemes and the ability to create a custom look.

Saving, Sharing and Presenting a Prezi

The free version of Prezi lets you create public presentations and share them online. You can also download a portable version and a PDF. For $59 a year, you can keep your Prezis private, and $159 gets you the software to create Prezis without an Internet connection.

Prezi lovers rejoiced when they allowed online collaboration. (I guess that's because they're hard to do so you want to divide the work . . . oh, that's a little snarky.)

5 Things to Know About Prezi

1. Prezi is an innovative way to present information and update boring PowerPoints.

2. The video camera-centric format is unique in that it allows you to share a "big picture" before you zoom in on the small details.

3. Prezi has a very open community that allows the sharing of templates and free use of the software. Paid versions start at $59 a year. You can buy templates or custom Prezis from freelancers and design companies.

4. Prezi can take a little while to master; but once you have the concept down, your presentations may be forever elevated.

5. The animation effects from all the zooming and turning and flying may make your attendees a little dizzy. Just sayin'.

Prezi Alternatives

Well, there's nothing really like Prezi out there right now, but here are some interesting ways to present your info without using PowerPoint.

- **Slidebean**
  slidebean.com

  Slidebean is a smart, clean presentation tool for online slideshows. Instead of starting with blank slides, Slidebean asks you to first organize your content (quotes, pictures, bullet points, etc.). Once you have an outline, Slidebean applies your chosen theme and creates a polished presentation. Free in beta, Slidebean is easy to use but with limited design options.

- **Emaze**
  emaze.com

  You will love the innovative templates with this Prezi/PowerPoint-type mashup. You create the presentations on the website, but a paid subscription will let you download your presentation and give your talk offline.

- **Sway**
  sway.com

  Believe it or not, one of the coolest new PowerPoint alternatives comes from . . . the creator of PowerPoint. Yes, indeed. Microsoft released Sway in 2014. This sleek presentation tool lets you create a program that's more like a flowing website. You can use it in place of traditional slides or let it stand alone. The challenge is that you'll have to be connected to the web to present.

- **Haiku Deck**
  haikudeck.com

  Haiku Deck provides beautiful, easy-to-use templates for presentations on the iPad and the web. The clean look of the templates is perfect for the minimalist design trends we see in today's best presentations.

- **Projeqt**
  projeqt.com

  Give your presentations dynamic content such as Twitter feeds with Projeqt. The tool intrigues me; but as a former English teacher, the spelling of the name gives me fits.

- **Bunkr**
  bunkrapp.com

  As of March 2015, Bunkr was still very much in beta, but it's making quite a splash. Like Projeqt, the standout feature is its ability to pull in live social media elements and websites to keep your presentation new and dynamic.

- **Keynote**
  keynote.com

  Keynote is Apple's version of PowerPoint with a cheaper price point and very hip transitions and templates.

Three Tools for Cooler Presentations

Take it from me—attendees want to do more than just sit there and listen to you blabber on. Use technology to add interactions and energy.

1. **Poll Everywhere**
   polleverywhere.com

   Let your attendees chime in via text with Poll Everywhere, and show the results in real-time on the screen (free for up to 25 responses).

2. **Electric Slide**
   electricslide.net

   Your attendees can follow along on their devices slide by slide as you present your PowerPoint with your iOS device. The bummer is that you're limited to five viewers in the free version and just 50 in the paid.

3. **KiwiLive**
   kiwilive.com

   I am a little bit biased toward this tool because I've been with it from the start and the owner, Jeff Mason, is pretty awesome. Upload a PDF of your presentation to let audience members follow along, and capture their email info for instant connections to your email newsletters and social media. I share bonus material with KiwiLive audiences, and the format lets me add a handsome link to my book. KiwiLive also has a live event feature that acts more or less like Poll Everywhere.

Nerd Know-How: Engage Live Audiences with Interactive Polls

Some presenters make great use of interactive technology in sessions, and some fall flat. If you're going to poll your audience, make sure you're incredibly clear with your instructions and give your audience members time to figure out how to text, vote or otherwise interact. I've had first-time texters feel triumphant when they send in a vote, and I've seen members of an audience get frustrated when "everyone else" understands what to do. If I have 100 audience members, I'll generally see from 30 to 60 votes on a Poll Everywhere activity.

Another thing to remember with interactive technology is that you don't want people looking down at their devices throughout your session. Pepper your presentation with a combination of physical and technological interactions, and make sure the activities are short and relevant. People can sit and text on their phones at home. In a session, audiences show up to be with people and interact.

Design

Pixlr pixlr.com

● ●

It's a well-known fact that if you need to crop an ex-boyfriend out of the family Christmas picture, your best option is **Adobe Photoshop**. The software used to be hundreds of dollars, but with **Adobe's Creative Cloud** monthly subscription, you can get Photoshop bundled with **Lightroom** for about 10 bucks a month. But even though Adobe tools are now in the realm of affordable, free is better.

Pixlr is my favorite online image editor, with a Flash-based uploader that allows you to edit from any computer without software. Pixlr is incredibly amazing, easy to use, fast, convenient and awesome. Does that make it clear how I feel?

From the Pixlr homepage, you can choose from three Pixlr online products. Pixlr's Express version is perfect for easy, immediate editing. It also has a fun Instagram-type filter and morphing tool, Pixlr-o-matic, which you can get online and on smart devices.

This section will focus on Pixlr Editor, which has many of the same features as Photoshop. All the tools you don't know how to use in Photoshop, you won't be able to figure out here either. It's that good.

I'd be pretty much a poser if I tried to give you master tricks to become an expert in Pixlr. Truth is, I only use a teeny-tiny fraction of its capabilities. But the things I use it for meet my needs and make my life easier.

Change Canvas Size

I often need to change the shape of a graphic to use it in a Generator (Page 167) or other graphics. If you change the size of the canvas in Pixlr, you can make the graphic any size you want.

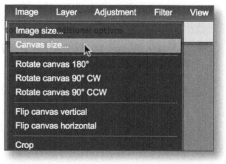

Pixlr Canvas Menu

From the Image Menu, choose the Canvas size option, and a dialog box pops up.

1. Type the width and height you need into the boxes.

2. Choose where you want the image to appear on the graphic. I generally center it inside the canvas, which means the extra space will be around my main graphic.

Canvas Size Dialog Box

Select Areas of an Image

One of the things that used to confound a non-designer like me is the mystery of the selection tools. A selected area will have dancing white lines around it. If some things are selected and some aren't, using tools like the eraser will only work in the selected areas. This can be very annoying. I've come to love the CTRL+D shortcut that deselects every-thing. You can also hold down the shift key and choose several sections at once rather than one at a time.

Here are four options for selecting areas.

Pixlr Select Tools

1. **Crop Tool** (top left)
   When you use this tool, you're selecting a portion of the graphic to keep. The rest will be discarded.

2. **Move Tool** (top right)
   Once an area is selected, use this tool to move the area somewhere else.

3. **Marquee Tool** (bottom left)
   The Marquee Tool is pretty straightforward. Click and drag over an area to select a square area.

4. **Lasso Tool** (bottom right)

   This tool makes me feel like a drunken artist. Click here and hold to draw a (never precise) line around your area. It'll complete itself if you don't go back to the beginning. I've never figured out how to make the Lasso select what I want. Guess that's why I was never a cowgirl.

Nerd Know-How: Understand Layers

The beauty of design software is the ability to modify every little part of your image. But I don't know how many hours I wasted before I figured out that Photoshop and its competitors create graphics out of layers, and you have to select the right layer to edit the stuff on it. Every time you add text or paste a graphic, you're adding another layer, and your original image may be set as the background. If you're clicking on stuff and it's not working, check to make sure you have selected the right layer.

Pixlr Layers

Design

NerdHerd Thumbs Up: PicsArt upgrades your mobile photography

Katie Ryan-Anderson, a NerdHerder from Northern Plains Electric Cooperative, recommends PicsArt (picsart.com) for editing and creating great graphics on the go for the online artistic community.

Take the Background Out of an Image

The little magic Wand Tool is by far my favorite. The Wand is the key to taking out a background on a graphic and making that area transparent so you don't paste an image with a big white box around it.

1. The Wand tool gives you a sparkly little stick that will choose an area based on color.

2. The keys to fine-tuning how much it chooses and how it does so are hidden in these three settings. The tolerance level has to do with how much variation the tool addresses. For example,

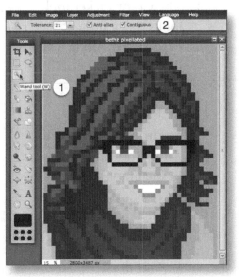

Wand Tool

you may have a white background for a picture of a guy with a white shirt. The shirt will likely be a few shades different from the white background. Setting the tolerance low will help you limit the selection to the white background color.

The anti-alias feature plays around with the pixels around the edges of your image. If it's selected, Pixlr will average out the surrounding pixels for a smoother look, rather than a pixelated border.

If you want to choose all of one color in the whole image, uncheck the Contiguous setting so the Wand will select all instances of that color.

Match Colors with Color Picker

This is another handy tool. The Color Picker loads colors from your image into your palette so you can use the colors elsewhere. I use it a lot when I am adding text to an image to make sure the color of the words matches the original.

1. The Color Picker tool looks like a little eyedropper. Gotta love that.

2. When you click the tool, your little eyedropper can grab a color from anywhere in the graphic.

3. Pixlr will save a palette of your recent color choices for easy switching.

Color Picker Tool

Fill an Area with Color

When I select something, I usually either delete it to make that area transparent, or I fill it with another color. That's why the Paint Bucket tool is another handy feature.

1. The Paint Bucket tool is a cute little—get this—paint bucket.

2. When you click the Paint Bucket over a selected area, the color or pattern in the palette spreads throughout the area.

3. You can play with fine-tuning settings similar to the Wand tool's options.

4. The color in your palette will be your paint.

Figure Paint Bucket Tool

4 Things to Know About Pixlr

1. Pixlr lets you edit images with Photoshop-type tools via apps and online.

2. As with Photoshop, some of the advanced editing tools that Pixlr offers may have higher learning curves.

3. The Wand tool is your secret weapon for removing backgrounds. Use the Wand tool to select the background of an object to delete. Then save the graphic as a PNG file to maintain the transparency.

4. Pixlr has quicker graphic editing options with its other tools and apps: Pixlr-O-Matic and Pixlr Express.

Pixlr Alternatives

- **GIMP**
  gimp.org

  GIMP was created in the mid-1990s and might be the king when it comes to open-source Adobe Photoshop competitors. Today a community of GIMP enthusiasts work together to upgrade the program, release new versions and get the word out. Download GIMP to manipulate photos with its many plug-ins and extensions, and visit the forums for lively and informative conversations about tips and bug fixes. Well, lively conversations for nerds.

NerdHerd Thumbs Up: GIMP is almost as good as Photoshop

Both Michael Shaw and Samantha Greasley love GIMP for image manipulation. Michael says, "It's nearly as good as Photoshop, only it's free, which makes it better!"

NerdHerd Thumbs Up: Adobe Shape creates quick vectors

Dawn James is a graphic designer and loves Adobe Shape (adobe.com/products/shape.html), a free iOS app that lets you snap pictures from your device and transform them into vectors without distortion.

- **Pixelmator**
  pixelmator.com

  On my Mac, my go-to Photoshop equivalent is Pixelmator if I need to work on something for a while instead of needing just a quick fix on Pixlr. I was thrilled when Pixelmator came out with an iPad app to bring the full feature set to a tablet. Apple named the iPad app the Best App of 2014.

- **Inkscape**
  inkscape.org

  For advanced printing projects, you may need a more robust tool. Most digital graphic files are sized to look great on the screen but aren't high-enough resolution to print well at a decent size. That's why your designer for a print project will often ask for vector files, which can be increased in size without loss of quality, instead of JPEGs, which can't.

Inkscape is a free open-source vector editor and is considered a worthy competitor for Adobe Illustrator. Don't even ask me how to use it—it's way beyond my humble graphic skills.

Eight Ways to Make Graphic Quotes

As wonderful as Pixlr is, you have to start from scratch to make beautiful graphics. These sites and apps provide shortcuts and templates to create social media-worthy images in a few clicks.

1. **Behappy.me**
   behappy.me/generator

   This quick-and-easy site lets you create a bright, clear message in a few clicks.

Pinterest Quote from Behappy.me

2. **Keep Calm-o-matic**
   keepcalm-o-matic.co.uk

   There are lots of imitators but only one original. Here's where you can make those awesome Keep Calm signs.

3. **Quozio**
   quozio.com

   Never lose a great quote again with this easy site. Just enter the quote and add the author, then choose from a dozen+ backgrounds and formats.

4. Pinstamatic
pinstamatic.com

This charming retro site lets you create quotes, maps, dates, pictures, sticky notes and more—all perfect for pinning with a couple of clicks.

5. Recite
recite.com

One of my favorite quick tools with dozens of instant templates for your sayings.

6. QuotesCover.com

This site doesn't have many options for fine-tuning, but you'll find plenty of ready-made templates for social media covers.

7. WordSwag
wordswag.co

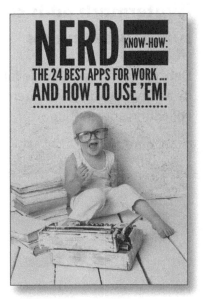

Oh my goodness but I love WordSwag! It's one of my favorite on-the-go tools to add a little somethin'-somethin' to my social media posts. When I announced the title of my new book, I used WordSwag to format it with this cute picture of a nerdy kid. The thing that makes this tool so cool is that the text comes in formatted, and you don't have to have an eye for design to create a fancy quote.

WordSwag Quote

It kills me to say that WordSwag is only available on iOS devices. I am still hunting for a great Android equivalent.

9. Over
   madewithover.com

   Although Over doesn't give you the preformatted awesomeness of WordSwag, its beautiful interface and limitless options make it a fun app to play with.

NerdHerd Thumbs Up: iWatermark adds copyright symbols to images

Debbi Haddaway is a huge fan of iWatermark (plumamazing.com) for its ability to easily add watermarks to the images you spend time collecting and crafting.

Canva

I had a tough time picking out an "easier than Photoshop" graphic tool to share because it is a close call between veteran tool **PicMonkey** (Page 122) and upstart **Canva**. Canva wins out because it seems to be keenly in tune with the types of graphics that we need to make in a flash, such as Facebook timeline photos, business cards and quick newsletter graphics.

Non-artistic folks like me need templates and simple instructions to create professional-looking graphics, and Canva is just the thing. The site provides modern and retro frameworks for everything from Facebook timeline images to presentation slides to business cards. It takes just a few minutes to make a badge, invitation or poster with a few clicks of the mouse—perfect for small-business folks who just need a quick graphic for a newsletter, social media post or website.

NerdHerd Thumbs Up:
Canva is super easy

Holly Duckworth and Lisa ONeill both put Canva on top of their favorite tool lists because it's simple, easy, affordable and "produces a great end product" within minutes.

Creating a Graphic

The first thing I love about Canva is right on the home page: the ability to pick quick templates for common graphics needs with just a click. It's constantly updating the templates, so if a social media site comes out with a new requirement for graphics, Canva gets you going.

Canva Home Page

Once you choose a template, your options are unlimited. Scroll through hundreds of pre-formatted layouts, or start fresh. Everything is adjustable, and the variety of fonts and filter overlays that give you a professional look instantly.

Canva lets you upload your own graphics or choose from both free and paid stock images. In the example on the next page, I searched for nerds; and within a couple of minutes, I customized its layout to make this mock magazine page. When you see hatch marks over a graphic, you have to cough up a buck to use it. Its stock images come from many of the royalty-free sites that I use such as 123RF (Page 125), and you'll pay much less on Canva than you will from the original sites, although you won't own the original image like you would if you purchased directly from a royalty-free site.

Canva Design Options

4 Things to Know About Canva

1. Canva is an easy way to create professional-looking graphics for websites, newsletters, social media graphics and more.

2. Canva is free to use. The service makes money selling high-quality backgrounds and images for your graphics for a buck each. The images it sells are generally cheaper than you'll pay buying the graphics yourself directly from the original source.

3. You'll be amazed at the templates and graphics they offer, as well as how fast they offer it. If a new social media trend takes hold, check Canva for the perfect-sized templates to set up your profile. They seem to know what graphics you need before you do.

4. Right now Canva seems to get new users by word of mouth—we nerds whisper our astonishment at its awesomeness when we're talking graphics. The service rapidly moved from beta testing into full-service mode, and in 2015 launched Canva for Work as a service for businesses.

Canva Alternative

- **PicMonkey**
  picmonkey.com

  When you check out PicMonkey, you'll see how hard it was for me to choose between it and Canva. Before Canva, my first online image creator love was Picnik. I never really got over it when Google bought it in 2010. But in 2012, two of the original engineers from Picnik started PicMonkey, another fun, free, fantastically easy online photo-editing site.

  As with Canva, PicMonkey has many user-friendly tools to resize, revamp and re-engineer a graphic in minutes. You can also find helpful tools to make your teeth whiter and add a little color to your cheeks. (I haven't seen anything out there that automatically eliminates extra chins. Let me know if you find one.)

  PicMonkey has a robust free version that is supported with ads; or you can upgrade for $33 per year for no ads and more effects, fonts and other goodies. It calls its upgrade the Royale level, and the little monkey gets a crown. I'm a sucker for that cute stuff.

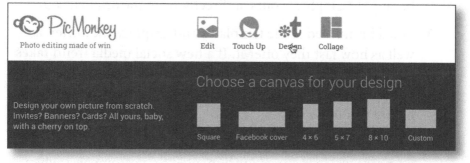

PicMonkey Home Page

Two Email Newsletter Platforms

Awesome graphics are great to spice up your newsletters. For many years, we've heard that email is dead for marketing; but in truth, sending newsletters and mass updates via email is still a valuable way to reach your audiences. You can choose from any number of robust do-it-yourself email blast senders, but often the rivalry comes down to two giants: Constant Contact and MailChimp.

1. **Constant Contact**
   constantcontact.com

   Constant Contact is a great choice for do-it-yourself newsletters. It has a wide variety of templates, and its tracking is robust and reliable. Pricing starts at $20 a month for up to 500 contacts, then Constant Contact get a little greedy with add-ons, charging more for events, surveys and more Facebook integrations.

   The major problem I have with Constant Contact (besides the price) is its a/b testing capabilities. It doesn't have any. To test a subject line, you have to manually break up your contact list and send to each group separately.

2. **MailChimp**
   mailchimp.com

   MailChimp is slightly less expensive and a whole lot more playful than Constant Contact. There is a free version with basic features for up to 2,000 contacts. After that, the pricing is quite comparable to Constant Contact and other rivals.

Nerd Know-How

Like Constant Contact, MailChimp has drag-and-drop templates that let you get pretty fancy with your designs. But what I really fall in love with is the automated a/b testing features for subject lines, sending times and more. You can write two subject lines and choose to send to a percentage of your list. Then you can let MailChimp pick a winner by either clickthrough or open rate, or you can determine which one performed the best. I've been able to increase the effectiveness of my campaigns by up to 10 percent by running tests.

123RF

123rf.com

Way back in the day, when small-business folks like me needed a nice image for our blogs, marketing or other stuff, we were forced to either, umm, borrow an image we found on the web (which was often low-resolution, thus bad for printing) or pony up hundreds for royalty-free stock photography from high-end sites such as **Getty Images** (Page 129).

But nowadays, there's no end to the number of so-called microstock sites—online marketplaces where freelance photographers and multimedia artists, both amateur and professional, sell their images for a fraction of the cost at the high-end sites.

The strangely named **123RF** is my favorite site. Most of my nerd pics come from here. Pricing starts at a couple of bucks per image. When I needed to create a larger library of nerd images, I paid $89 a month for a while to download up to five images a day. The same graphics show up on other sites for three to five times the price.

Finding the Right Image

Microstock sites such as 123RF are huge, with a kabillion photos, vectors, video clips and audio. There are so many sites that it may feel like it would be easier to go outside and take the picture yourself than to find the perfect image.

Royalty-Free Image from
Release Your Inner Nerd

Nerd Know-How

You can start with a general search, then when you see the types of files that are out there, narrow down your results with its fine-tuning tools (123RF Search Options, Page 126). When you click on an image or file you like, you'll see purchasing options as well as keyword tags, a link to the artist's portfolio, more pictures of the same model as well as a collection of similar stock photos. These are all great ways to get the right file.

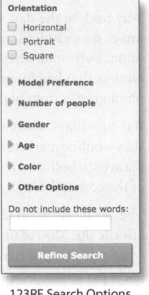

When I'm gathering a bunch of images, I create a lightbox to collect them. On 123RF, you can add images from a search just by clicking a little heart on each image. If you're working with a team, you can send the lightbox to them. I've used lightboxes to pick out images for a website during a redesign. I just send the lightbox with my choices to my designer who purchases the ones that work best for our vision.

123RF Search Options

You can also broaden your search to include more royalty-free sites and compare prices.

Stock Image Nerd Search

Design

My favorite way to do this is through **Google Image Search**. First I include the word "stock" in some form or fashion in the search, such as "stock image nerd."

In Chrome browsers, you can simply drag an image from a search into the search bar, and in other browsers you'll find a link to Search by Image when you click on an image in the gallery.

Google Search by Image

Other Search Engine's Image Search

When you get the results from your image search, you'll find similar images. In this case, this nerd is available on at least two different microstock sites, so you can compare prices.

Google Image Search Results

Four Things to Know About 123RF

1. Microstock sites such as 123RF offer royalty-free files such as images, audio and video at budget-friendly prices.

2. 123RF pricing per image ranges from a buck to dozens of dollars. If you need lots of images, a monthly subscription might be less expensive than individual credits.

3. Study the fine print for the licenses. Most of the time, a standard license will work. A standard license covers my needs for the cover of my second book, *Release Your Inner Nerd*, as long as I don't sell more than 50,000 copies. Heck, if I sell 50,000 copies of my books, I'd HIRE that nerd to jump for me.

4. You can't use the images in your logo, in a way that degrades the models or to resell as your own. In other words, be cool with the images, dude.

123RF Alternatives

*   **Microstock Sites**
    You won't believe the number of microstock sites for royalty-free files. A few of the ones I've used:

    *   **iStockphoto** (istockphoto.com)

    *   **Dreamstime** (dreamstime.com)

    *   **Shutterstock** (shutterstock.com)

    *   **Depositphotos** (depositphotos.com)

    *   **Fotolia** (fotolia.com)

    *   **Stockfresh** (stockfresh.com)

- **Vectors and Illustrations**
  Check out **Clipart Of, VectorStock** and **CartoonStock** for, well, clipart, vectors and cartoons. (clipartof.com, vectorstock.com and cartoonstock.com)

- **Free Sites**
  You'll have to read the fine print on the licenses for these free images, but check out **Flickr Creative Commons** (flickr.com/creativecommons), **Morguefile** (morguefile.com) and **Wikimedia Commons** (commons.wikimedia.org) to start. But be careful—just because they're available doesn't mean the person who put them up there has permission to share them. Another cool site is **Unsplash.com**, which shares incredibly beautiful, high-res photographs that are perfect for inspirational quotes (see great quote tools, Page 116).

- **Envato Marketplace**
  envato.com

  Envato is a collection of freelance design sites that allow you to buy royalty-free everything, from audio clips to images to PowerPoint designs to every electronic template you might ever need. I have purchased templates for websites, presentations and printed material, as well as little add-ons for WordPress (Page 201) and more.

Nerd Know-How: Upgrade Your Look with Getty Images

With everyone in the world stealing Getty Images (gettyimages.com) from the web, the company gave up the fight somewhat. Getty now lets you embed many of its images on your site using its code—for free.

Five Ways to Make Photo Books

Whether you're creating a professional book with product images for work or a family album to treasure forever, these photo book services make the process easy and the product memorable.

1. **GrooveBook**
   groovebook.com

   I've talked before about things you can do with cool photos from your mobile devices, but one of my favorite projects is to turn phone photos into keepsake albums for a few dollars and with even fewer clicks. For GrooveBook, just choose up to 100 photos per month, and once a month you'll receive an adorable little book with perforated photos to share—for just $2.99 per month, including shipping.

2. **Mosaic**
   heymosaic.com

   This beautiful hardcover photo album is a bit pricy at $25, but it's an elegant way to showcase 20 phone pictures in a gift-ready package. The name comes from the mosaic look of the beautiful peek-a-boo cover.

3. **Shutterfly**
   shutterfly.com

   My sister uses Shutterfly to share pics of my adorable nephews, and as well she should. This site is a safe place for schools and families to share kid photos, plus it has a robust series of tools to create photo books and gifts. Shutterfly is more expensive than other options (such as Kindred at $7.99, for example), but my sister tells me the site is generous with coupons, and you can always check **RetailMeNot.com** for discount codes. FYI, Shutterfly bought GrooveBook in November 2014.

4. **Postagram** and 5. **Felt**
sincerely.com/postagram and **feltapp.com**

You can find a whole bunch of apps that let you send real mail from your mobile device. With super-thick postcards with a picture that pops out, Postagram is my favorite. Felt goes a little further. In late 2014 the company introduced Storyframes, a feature that lets you choose several pictures to send in an accordion-fold format. The cards are beautiful, and their square shape makes them hip (as in "it's hip to be square"). You can choose to send up to four pictures for a maximum of $6 (including U.S. postage).

NerdHerd Thumbs Up:
DealNews brings sales to you

NerdHerder Laura Young loves DealNews (dealnews.com), a service that gathers all the great sales and discounts in one place for easy shopping. Other nerds swear by the RetailMeNot apps, which alert you to discounts when you are near a retail store with a sale.

Dafont

dafont.com

• •

When it comes to the look and feel of a document, changing the font can change the personality. **Dafont** is my very favorite place on the web to find fonts with pizazz to add a little something extra to a look.

Finding a Font

The key to finding your perfect font on Dafont is to put sample text into the custom preview box and then search by theme (cartoon, curly, calligraphy, handwritten). Most are free for personal use, and many are just plain free.

Dafont Details

Dafont Preview Pane

1. The fonts are broken down into themes. Choose any theme, and you'll get a preview box.

2. Type in your sample text into the Preview field and click submit. You can now see a preview of all fonts with your text.

3. When you expand more options to the right of the Submit button, you can eliminate the fonts that are free only for personal use. You should also always read the "Read Me" file in the font download folder to see what rights a font designer gives you.

4. Click the download button and save the font ZIP file to your computer. When you double click on a font, your computer should guide you through the installation process.

Nerd Know-How: Watch Out for Unusual Fonts

You may have an awesome font called "Chicken Butt" on your computer (yes, there is such a thing), but your recipients probably won't. Either embed the fonts into a PDF or create a graphic out of your word with a screenshot (Page 84).

3 Things to Know About Dafont

1. Dafont is a massive database of free and bargain fonts that you can download onto your computer and use in documents and graphics.

2. Dafont helps you visualize your creative ideas with custom previews and themes. You can also download graphic fonts that substitute little pictures (dingbats and wingdings and webdings, oh my!).

3. Most of the fonts are free for personal use, but you'll have to use filters to find ones you can use commercially. Read the fine print on fonts you use for work—the guidelines for use vary greatly.

Dafont Alternatives

- **Font Squirrel**
  fontsquirrel.com

  Font Squirrel is another great resource, though it doesn't let you preview your text. The cool thing about the resources on this site is that they're all free for commercial use, so you won't have the letdown of finding the perfect font and then having to give it up because it's only for personal use.

- **FontSpace**
  fontspace.com

  FontSpace offers great diversity and free fonts for personal and business use.

- **Kevin and Amanda**
  kevinandamanda.com

  How cute! This site specializes in adorable handwriting tools. They're mostly for scrapbook enthusiasts, but they can be handy for notes with that handwritten look.

- **Google Web Fonts**
  google.com/fonts

  If you're looking to add a little snazzy-ness to your website, you can find new fonts that will work on the web at Google Web Fonts.

Four Ways to Find the Right Font

Eureka! You've discovered the perfect font for your next marketing piece on a political postcard that arrived in the mail. But what's the font's name, and where can you find it? Or how do you determine what the font is going to look like on the screen? These tools will put you on the right track.

1. **Identifont**
   identifont.com

   Identifont has a step-by-step wizard that takes you through a series of questions about the font, such as where the squiggle goes on the capital "Q." It'll even help if you have only a few letters to work with (like a flier headline). Another great search engine is Identifont's picture search tool, which combs picture- and symbol-based fonts to help you find that perfect dingbat of a pair of nerdy glasses.

2. **WhatTheFont!**
   myfonts.com/whatthefont

   Now for the tool with the best name in this book: WhatTheFont! The site (and mobile app) will analyze a graphic of your mystery font and make recommendations. If you don't find a match, try visiting the WhatTheFont Forum, where it says, "Cloak-draped font enthusiasts around the world will help you out!"

3. **Typetester**
   typetester.org

   This site lets you really fine-tune the look of your text on a screen. You can compare up to three fonts and tweak their look to your heart's content. Frankly, if you spend more than 30 minutes on this site and you're not a website designer, you have a font addiction.

4. **Wordmark.it**

   Have you ever spent a half-hour in Microsoft Word scrolling through your installed fonts one by one to find the perfect look for a document? Wordmark.it is a clever web tool that lets you write a few words for a preview then loads your fonts into the site so you can see them all at once. The site lets you choose your favorites then filter them to see your top choices together. It's 100 percent free and super easy to use.

Wordmark.it

Create

Animoto

animoto.com

Once you read this section, you should tear it off and eat it so none of your co-workers or competitors ever learns the secret behind your seemingly effortless awesomeness. **Animoto** is one of those tools that make the crowds go "WOW" and look at you in wonder.

The premise is incredibly simple: Gather 10 or more pictures and/or videos, throw in a title and choose a theme and soundtrack—then push a button. PRESTO! Animoto instantly creates a perfectly timed, perfectly professional, perfectly awesome video that can showcase your event, your boss's retirement, your kid's prom preparations, your company's products—you name it. And when you share the video, your audience will whisper, "Wow, how did she do that?" It's won all kinds of awards including a Crunchie and a Webby, and you can even use it to create high-quality DVD videos.

Animoto is just plain cool, with an intuitive interface and fun graphics. The service is free for a very simple 30-second video, but the lowest paid version is just $30 a year and gives you all kinds of extra functionality. These days it's pushing professional levels and the higher pricing via the website, so the best way to locate the lowest pricing is through the app.

Creating an Animoto

You can create an Animoto from the web or your mobile device, using pictures from any number of sources. If you start with the website, you'll work within the Animoto Create Menu.

1. You create a name for each video. On mobile devices, it'll name your video after your account by default—it calls all mine "Beth's Video." The mobile version also inserts the title and date

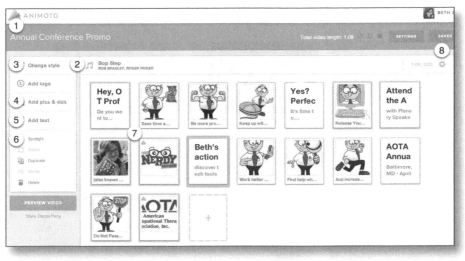

Animoto Create Menu

as a text card into the video by default, but you can modify the
text before you produce the final version.

2. The system will make a recommendation for a soundtrack
    based on the theme you choose. You have 2,000+ tracks to
    choose from if you want something different. You can also
    upload your own music if you own the rights.

3. The Change Style option lets you choose from dozens of pre-
    designed templates. This is where the real fun is. Here are a few
    of your options, ranging from very professional to romantic to
    whimsical. My best standbys are the Dance Party theme and the
    Animoto Original. I also like Inkwell, but it's a little dark.
    Birthday Gifts can be quite fun, even for a non-birthday
    occasion.

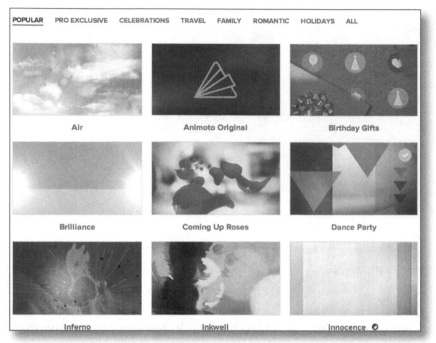

POPULAR   PRO EXCLUSIVE   CELEBRATIONS   TRAVEL   FAMILY   ROMANTIC   HOLIDAYS   ALL

Air — Animoto Original — Birthday Gifts

Brilliance — Coming Up Roses — Dance Party

Inferno — Inkwell — Innocence

Animoto Style Selection

Nerd Know-How:
Pick an Animoto Theme

Some of the themes are more forgiving with unusual image sizes than others. They'll let you move the center of your picture somewhat to fit a theme's frame, but you could end up with cropped pictures where you wanted the whole image.

4. You can upload pics and video from your computer, or just choose images from your library on the mobile apps. Video clips are limited to 10 seconds in the lower-priced versions.

Nerd Know-How: Add Video to Animoto

If you have a longer video clip you really want to play, duplicate the video and choose consecutive clips from each. I did this once when I captured a group of nerds singing *You've Lost That Loving Feeling.* You can also edit your video clips and mute the sound so the soundtrack plays consistently through your video.

5. A great way to organize your video is to add text slides. You can also put captions on the pictures, but the captions have different effects in different styles, and some are harder to read than others.

6. The Spotlight option rocks! Just click the star, and the picture or text will get another second or so of screen time. This helps you control the pacing of your video and gives your audience a chance to read or digest a detailed section.

7. Animoto helps you create a high-quality video by putting little warning signs on low-resolution images that may turn out fuzzy.

8. The Settings option lets you control the song length and the slide pacing.

Edit song and pacing

SONG TRIM

▶ 3:02

IMAGE PACING

MANUAL ⬤ AUTO ❓

SLOW ● FAST

Save

Animoto Pacing Options

Nerd Know-How: Make Videos on the Fly at a Conference

The mobile apps (Android and iOS) make the tool even more awesome at a conference or meeting. Snap pictures of conference exhibitors for a dynamic thank-you video at the closing session, or make a montage on the fly of the award winners from your luncheon. Everything you need to produce the video is on your mobile device, and it takes just minutes to render. Because I frequently pick the same styles and soundtracks, I can create a whole video in less than 2 minutes. My record is 92 seconds. #nerdpride

5 Things to Know About Animoto

1. Animoto takes your photos and short videos and synchronizes them into a multimedia movie complete with a soundtrack.

2. The mobile apps let you take a handful of photos at an event and have a professional-level video within minutes. No, really. Minutes.

3. You can share your Animoto videos via social media or upload to YouTube with one click.

4. Use features such as title slides and Spotlight to guide people through your video and to enhance certain features.

5. If you're using the video in a large presentation room, you can download an HD version for larger screens for $5-$10. (Upgrades are free with higher-priced subscriptions.)

NerdHerd Thumbs Up:
Everyone loves Animoto

When I asked the NerdHerd members to share their favorite tech tools, Animoto was one of the most popular, listed by Donna Kendrena and three others. Brett Hanft says Animoto is a creative and fun way to make a point. Cheryl from In-Joy Travel says it's fun to play with and loves the results. And Loretta Peskin incudes Animoto videos in her union newsletter.

Animoto Alternatives

- **Magisto**
  magisto.com

  I've been playing around with this instant moviemaker, and I'm more or less impressed. Although it doesn't have nearly the number of options as Animoto, Magisto does a great job with video clips and makes a cool instant movie. Sometimes, though, it focuses on a strange spot, and I've generated a lot of movies with close-ups of nostrils and chins. A new feature called CamCrew helps you improve your videotaping skills to make an even better movie. The free version of Magisto gives you a little more time than Animoto's, and the next levels start at $30 a year.

- **Flipagram**
  flipagram.com

  Use your Instagram pictures or your photo library to create short, punchy videos with a lot of energy. This one doesn't add any cool transitions or special effects, but it's free and very popular.

- **Videolicious**
  videolicious.com

  This innovative app lets you make a very cool voiceover video for a collection of pictures and video clips in minutes. Just choose the clips and pictures, hit the record button, then scroll through your media and record a voiceover for the selections. Unfortunately Videolicious just switched from a simple subscription plan to mysterious Enterprise pricing for more professional videos. I asked several times for a ballpark estimate of costs, and the response was, "I'm not at liberty to say." The Personal level still lets you make 1-minute videos for free.

- **iMovie**
  apple.com/imovie

  Sorry to bring up yet another Apple-only product, but if you're playing around with homemade videos, you have to play with iMovie. The app includes easy-to-use transitions, templates and treatments to turn raw videos into polished segments.

  My favorite iMovie trick is to use one of the "coming attractions" templates to create what looks like a movie trailer. The templates tell you *exactly* what to shoot, with segment titles such as "Group" and "Two Shot" and "Action Shot." I made a superhero princess video with my little cousin in about 15 minutes, and it took me just 45 minutes to do one with my cats (their names are Copy and Paste). The little girl took direction much better than my kitties. The mobile app has fewer templates than the Mac version, but it's super cool to be able to create an entire video from your phone in minutes.

Nerd Know-How:
Create Engaging Videos for Social Media

Perhaps you're asking yourself what your business would do with a tool that makes superhero princess movie trailers. In this social media world, people love companies and organizations with personalities. Maybe you make an adventure movie trailer with your board of directors as they set off on a retreat to rethink your organization's vision. Or you could capture the antics of your staff for a friendly holiday video for your clients. Or you could even showcase your newest products with a fun intro video. You'll be surprised how an engaging video can enhance your relationship with your customers—just try it!

Five Ways to Make Animated Videos

You know those awesome explainer videos that startup companies with marketing budgets create to showcase their products? Design companies charge thousands to create these custom videos, but now they have strong competition from a host of animate-it-yourself video generators.

1. **PowToon**
   powtoon.com

   PowToon is a pioneer in low-cost animation generators. The service lets you use easy-to-manipulate figures to create your own videos. It takes a little finagling to get used to the interface; but once you understand the basics, you can create a brag-worthy showstopper. You can create PowToon-branded videos and slides for free, or buy a subscription starting at $19 per month for an annual plan. You can also keep the free version and just pay a few bucks to upgrade your video to HD. NerdHerder Joe Ferri gives PowToon bonus points for ease of use.

2. **Wideo**
   wideo.co

   Wideo is very similar to PowToon in terms of video controls and a handful of templates. Choose from pay-as-you-go options and a subscription.

3. **GoAnimate**
   goanimate.com

   GoAnimate has a template-based video creator as well and some really cool, granular settings that will help you create something special. GoAnimate's pricing is a little bit higher, and

I didn't pay for a membership to try it out. I'm not good enough at these things to invest a lot of time and money if I'm not going to use it. I usually outsource my videos to Fiverr (Page 192) where there are plenty of experts who can do the work in no time.

4. **Adobe Voice**
   getvoice.adobe.com

   Adobe threw a cool tool into the video world in 2014 with Adobe Voice. This iPad-only app lets you search for stock images or upload your own. Then you record voiceovers for each slide in an incredibly easy process. Once you have your video, you can change the theme and add a soundtrack. When you finish your video, Adobe uploads all the credits for the images and music you chose from its collection.

   The bummer about Adobe Voice (besides the fact that it's iPad only) is that you can't download the video, so you'll have to play it online.

5. **VideoScribe**
   videoscribe.co

   If you have nimble thumbs, you can drag and drop your way to a quality whiteboard animation on your mobile device. VideoScribe is available as an app or (more expensive) software download. I found the iPhone version a little hard to manipulate on the small screen, but it's still a pretty amazing tool. The professional version has several pricing options, from a one-time payment to a month-to-month subscription.

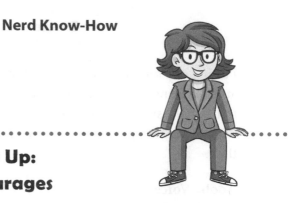

NerdHerd Thumbs Up:
Adobe Voice encourages
engagement

Amanda White says she loves Adobe Voice because of its ability to make clean, informational videos. "I use it to get information across regarding Call-to-Action items."

Piktochart

Thousands of people read my newsletter every week. Some editions are very popular; others are duds. But I don't take time to look at the big picture, or at least I didn't until MailChimp (Page 123) sent me an end-of-year review. My report contained analyses of my list growth, the best subject lines and the most active recipients. All of a sudden, the giant pile of statistics that my weekly newsletter generates was converted into tangible, comprehensible facts.

Infographics take on the job of converting big data into understandable ideas, and they're all the rage on social media. My first infographic was an analysis of the elements of the perfect nerdy office, which I put together with **Piktochart.** I have to tell you that it takes patience—a lot of patience. Elements jump around, move mysteriously, and are challenging to align and move. But the overall result of my first attempt was really quite pleasing. The free account is pretty basic, so if you're really into these things, you might want to pay the $29 a month for the Pro version.

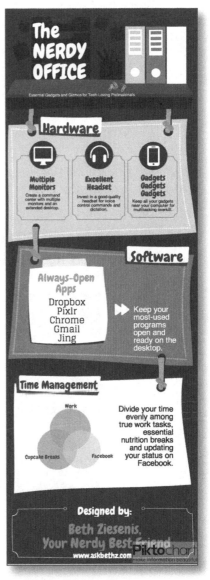

Piktochart Example

Using Piktochart

You'll enjoy the template options that Piktochart offers: You can create an infographic, a report, a banner or a presentation. Each has its own variations.

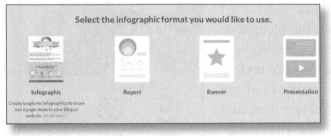

Piktochart Template Options

Once you choose a type of infographic, you get more template choices. You'll find five or six free templates, then a whole host of Pro options.

Piktochart Infographic Templates

Once you find the template you want to personalize, you get an online editor. Plug in your data to personalize the charts, or just change the titles and graphics. Here's where I got in trouble with elements jumping around and not fitting anymore, so you might want to make sure that your new text and graphic is approximately the same size as the placeholder.

Piktochart Online Editor

1. The graphic tool lets you add stock graphics.

2. With the free version, you can upload 20 of your own images. You get 200 with the paid version.

3. You can change the background into some interesting textures, but the free version again has a limit.

4. With a click of the styles button, you can choose a different color scheme.

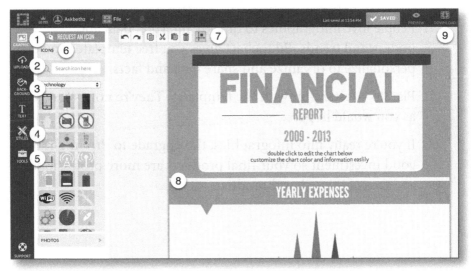

Piktochart Online Editor

5. Piktochart lets you add elements such as charts, maps and videos, which can make your graphic interactive.

6. You'll find more graphics than you would guess in the stock images library. It's easy to create a uniform look for your infographic with a series of similarly designed icons.

7. When you select an element, you get a host of tools to fine-tune the look.

8. Each infographic is divided into blocks, which you edit individually. This way you can control each area a little rather than pushing everything down or squishing up while you work on it.

9. You're limited to web-quality public graphics with the free version. The Pro version lets you download a high-res PDF and choose other privacy options.

3 Things to Know About Piktochart

1. People love infographics to quickly interpret data and understand trends. Piktochart gives you free templates you can personalize to organize and share data and facts.

2. Plan to wrestle a bit with the templates. They're not as forgiving as you would hope.

3. If you're really into infographics, the upgrade to Pro might be a good investment so your final products are more professional and free of Piktochart branding.

Nerd Know-How: Create a Useful Infographic

Like any infographic tool, Piktochart is best for 2-10 data points or facts. Don't get carried away with detail—aim for information that can be easily digested.

Piktochart Alternatives

- **Easel.ly**
  Easel.ly comes in a close second in the race for my favorite infographic tool. You can click on any of the infographics in the public gallery and make them your own.

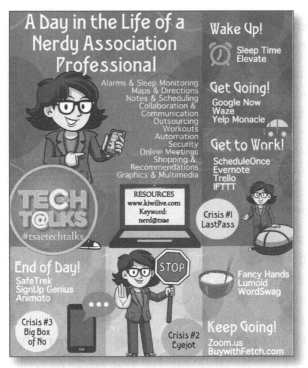

Easel.ly Infographic

- **Infogr.am**

  Infogr.am is another option, but the free version makes you work pretty hard to make the infographic beautiful. One cool feature is that it integrates with a tool called import.io, which extracts data from websites and puts it into spreadsheets. I didn't have the patience to make import.io work my first time out, but it seems like a very handy tool for people who need to grab lists and more from a site. Creep alert: Don't use import.io for evil by scraping contacts from sites to spam. That's uncool.

Four Tools for Teachers

Piktochart is a great tool for the classroom to help students visualize their research. Here are more helpful classroom tools.

1. **LiveBinders**
   livebinders.com

   Meeting planners, teachers and anyone with projects tend to collect binders of stuff on their desks. LiveBinders takes those resources to the digital world and lets you share them with others. You can also browse the hundreds of public binders full of great info.

2. **Remind**
   remind.com

   This tool was created for the world of education, but Remind has potential for other groups that need to connect via text. Remind asks teachers to set up group texting for designated classes. Students and parents sign up for the class updates, and instructors can send little notes about tomorrow's test or a new resource for homework. Everyone's phone numbers are kept confidential for both the broadcasts and one-to-one chats.

3. **Kahoot!**
   getkahoot.com

   Can't separate your students from their devices? Kahoot! is an audience response system designed for the classroom (but useful for businesses as well) with fun, interactive graphics and a video-game look.

4. **Glogster**
   glogster.com

   This poster-making tool almost made it into my second book, but I just wasn't sure about some of the weird sites it had available for referencing. But Glogster has cleaned out the riff and the raff. The rejuvenated Glogster site is amazing for helping students create interactive multimedia posters for classmates. Rejuvenation usually means re-pricing. Glogster's free version lets teachers set up an account for 10 students. Other levels start at $39 a year.

Tagxedo

tagxedo.com

Warning! Tagxedo Is an Endangered Species

Tagxedo is one of our favorite tools, but its days may be limited. It runs only on the web through Microsoft Silverlight technology, which the Chrome browser recently stopped supporting (it works on other browsers still). We thought about leaving Tagxedo out of this book because of its endangered status, but the NerdHerd voted to keep this section. Use it as long as you can because it's awesome.

Tagxedo

Create

No matter your profession, chances are you'll be able to find a use for a word cloud graphic, which takes words and concepts and transforms them into works of art. **Tagxedo** is my very favorite word cloud tool because of its flexibility. You can make a quick, traditional word collage in less than 5 minutes, or create a perfect masterpiece with umpteen customizations.

Tagxedo, like many word art sites, lets you upload a list of words or will analyze a document, site or pasted text. Depending on your settings, the most frequent words in your text will appear larger than the other words.

Tagxedo is an online-only web app that doesn't work on mobile devices or Chrome browsers because it runs on an older technology called Microsoft Silverlight. Tagxedo is free, even though the site threatens that some features are free only in the beta version. I wrote to the founder about any potential updates, and he didn't write back. That's always a bad sign.

Tagxedo Options

In just a couple of minutes, Tagxedo can help you create a social media graphic, but to really get the look you want, you may want to fine-tune the settings. These screenshots will help you understand the basics as well as the advanced features.

Tagxedo Main Menu

1. **Load**
   Paste your own text or list, upload a .txt file, or enter a website address.

2. **Save | Share**
   The site has lots of ways to keep and share your graphic, including social media and JPG and PNG files.

157

Note: Tagxedo is built with Microsoft Silverlight software, which doesn't work on mobile devices. Thus, don't bother trying to embed the interactive graphic into your site. Just save it as an image file and use it that way.

3. **Color**
   Once you choose a theme or set the colors, use this button to redistribute the color palette to the words.

4. **Theme**
   The site has a bunch of preset color schemes to choose from. You can also customize the colors, but it's a little complicated. I've never gotten it to work.

5. **Font**
   By default, the site will choose three random fonts for your graphic. This area lets you specify your favorites.

6. **Orientation**
   This option lets you choose whether the words are all vertical, all horizontal, a combination of both or random. I tend to use the combination horizontal/vertical setting the most because it seems to fill the edges of shapes the best.

7. **Layout**
   This option rearranges the location of words in your shape.

8. **All**
   My favorite button—press this to change all the other options. You can also lock a few of the settings (such as Font) and randomize the rest.

   Tip: Generate a bunch of random configurations at once by clicking this button multiple times in a row. Then you can view all the configurations in History and find your favorite starting point.

9. **Shape**

   Click here to choose from dozens of shape templates. Some of them are rather odd (such as Lincoln's head or the lowercase "t"). Here's where you upload your own shape and play with the areas that will be filled with words. You can also choose to fill a word with other words, or make the words leave a blank shape in the center of your graphic by clicking the Invert button.

Nerd Know-How: Use Your Own Image in Tagxedo

If you upload your own shape, choose "Use Source Color" in the Word | Layout Options >> Layout heading to keep the original colors. If your shape is a little hard to read, click the word "Shape," and Tagxedo inserts an outline of your object.

10. **History**

    Tagxedo doesn't let you save your masterpieces to work on later, but everything you've done in one session will be visible in your history.

11. **Word | Layout Options**

    This is where the magic can happen. Here's a breakdown of all the advanced options in this area.

Word Options Menu

1. **Punctuation**
   Be sure to allow punctuation if you have apostrophes and such, or your words will be separated and you'll end up with "don't" showing up as a "don" and a "t."

2. **Numbers**
   Choose "Yes" to allow digits.

3. **Remove Common Words**
   This controls whether words such as "the" and "a" will appear in your graphic.

Word Options Menu

4. **Combine Related Words**
   This option lets you choose whether the words "nerd" and "nerds" appear separately or combined.

5. **Combine Identical Words**
   If you have a bunch of the same exact word, you can choose whether Tagxedo sees them as one word with a lot of emphasis or a whole bunch of separate words.

6. **Frequency Modifier**
   This helps you determine just how much emphasis you want one word to have. For example, you could write "Nerd:15000" in this field to make it seem like the word "Nerd" occurs 15,000 times in your text and thus deserves a bigger representation. You'll need to set Normalize Frequency in the Layout menu to "Yes" to make this feature work. This is pretty complicated stuff. I just ignore it and play with the other buttons.

7. **Apply NonLatin Heuristics**

   Choose this option if you have non-Latin characters (such as Chinese symbols).

8. **Default Link**

   This determines what happens when you click on a word in the interactive version of the graphic. Don't bother with this because you don't want to embed interactive Tagxedos into your site because they're not compatible with mobile devices.

Layout Menu

1. **Emphasis**

   This slider determines the ratio between the biggest words and the smallest in your graphic. If you want words to stand out more, increase the percentage.

2. **Maximum Word Count**

   The default word count is 200, but by increasing the number of words, you may be able to fill in a shape more evenly.

Layout Options Menu

Nerd Know-How: Finding the Best Word Count for Tagxedo

I've found that Tagxedo handles 50-100 words pretty well. Upload a list with more than 100 words, and you run the risk that the words further down the list might not show up in the graphic. You can adjust this by not allowing replication and by playing with the maximum word count.

3. **Tightness**

   This setting is the key to really filling in a shape. Slide the Tightness setting higher to increase the amount of space that the words will fill.

4. **Color Variation**

   You can modify the amount of variation in the colors in any theme.

5. **Normalize Frequency**

   Play with this setting if you want to control which words will appear largest.

6. **Hard Boundary**

   This determines whether words can creep outside the shape's lines. Use it for more amorphous shapes or when you have longer words or phrases that might not fit if the boundaries don't have a little leeway.

7. **Use Source Color**
   If you have uploaded your own shape, such as a logo, choose to use the source color so your words take their color themes from the picture and retain the colors of the original shape. This is one of my favorite features for really personalizing a graphic.

8. **Allow Replication**
   Most of the time, you'll want to allow replication so that you'll have enough words to fill in the shape.

9. **Theme Preference**
   If you're randomly choosing color themes, you can limit your choices here to more quickly identify looks you prefer.

10. **Font Preference**
    Just like with Theme Preference, you can control the number of fonts the system will try to use.

Other Menus

1. **Skip Menu**
   The Skip Menu brings up a list of all the words in your graphic. You can choose to skip certain words and remix your cloud. These controls are very helpful if you've asked Tagxedo to analyze text for you. You can remove irrelevant words and leave the thoughts you want your Tagxedo to include.

2. **Advanced Menu**
   This area lets you alter the background color and opacity of your cloud. You can also use the Déjà vu feature to keep the same formatting on words as you compare two texts (such as two speeches). The Scatter slider spreads the words out in your shape.

Nerd Know-How:
Tweak a Tagxedo Word Cloud

Here's a classic example of how a little bit of advanced tweaking will give you a great graphic. I took a list of 40 of my favorite fictional nerds (how many do you recognize?), and uploaded them to create the word "NERDS." The first take looked like this:

Nerd Graphic Original

Obviously I wasn't going for the word "IERD." The main problem was that the words didn't fit the letters. The tools to fix the problem were in the Layout Menu.

I increased the Maximum Word Count to 300+ so I'd have more material to fill in the blank spaces. Then I slid the Tightness bar to the right to about 180%. I also played a little bit with the Emphasis slider, decreasing it a smidge so there was less variation in the word sizes. The changes decreased the blank spaces and filled in my graphic. The next version was perfect.

Nerd Graphic Adjusted

4 Things to Know About Tagxedo

1. Tagxedo is the coolest way out there to create word art.

2. The site and the embedded interactive graphics won't work on your mobile devices.

3. In April of 2015, the Chrome browser stopped supporting Microsoft Silverlight, which is used by about half of us Internet addicts. That means you'll have to use Internet Explorer, Firefox or Safari to access Tagxedo.

4. The most helpful tips are to use a tilde (~) instead of spaces to keep words together, and use the Tightness setting in the Layout Menu to get words to fill all the spaces of your shape.

Tagxedo Alternatives

*   **Wordle**
    wordle.net

    THE classic word art tool, Wordle is great for analyzing text. It doesn't have the options to create a shape or use multiple fonts, but Wordle doesn't suffer from the funky Microsoft Silverlight problems that Tagxedo has.

*   **Tagul**
    tagul.com

    You have to register to use Tagul, but this word-cloud generator works on mobile devices and has many fun ways to customize a cloud.

- **Cloudart**
  cloudart-app.com

  Cloudart is a beautiful app for iPads. It still isn't Tagxedo, though.

- **WordFoto** (iOS) and **WordCam** (Android)
  wordfoto.com and **WordCam** in the Google Play Store

  These awesome alternatives to traditional word clouds use words more like paint in your pictures. WordCam is a little old, but it still works. Buy the Pro version to get rid of the word "WordCam" in your art.

NerdHerd Thumbs Up: EVERYONE Loves Tagxedo

Tagxedo is another tool that showed up multiple times on the NerdHerd favorites list. Nora Y. Onishi and Liliana Donatelli both enjoy it because it conveys concepts of ideas in a single shape. Janet McEwen says, "It really jazzes up presentations and drives home a concept." Michele Huber agrees. "It's awesome. It's cute. It can make a personal art gift. It's free!"

Three (Plus) Graphic Generators

Although you may find that quote generators (Page 116) create the best viral content for social media, these quick graphic generators have their places. When I use these for business, I skip over the ones that are obvious copyright infringements, risqué or, well, bizarre. There are lots of those. For more tips on making a nice graphic with these tools, read about changing canvas size with Pixlr (Page 108).

1. **Photofacefun**
   Photofacefun.com

   This silly site is where I get most of my graphics for presentations because its Etch-A-Sketch graphic and the picture of the dog on the computer are real show-stoppers (or at least that is what I choose to believe).

Dog with Computer from PhotoFaceFun.com

2. **ImageChef**
   imagechef.com

   I have kind of a like/dislike relationship with ImageChef. On one hand, I see all these little templates that I think I'm going to love. But sometimes when I start making them, the cheese factor goes really high. Nonetheless, you can make cool images with pictures and

Nerd Stamp from ImageChef.com

text, and ImageChef's app is very fun to use. If you want to remove the watermark or get a higher-quality image, you'll have to pay for the Pro version, which is about $10 for a week or $100 for a year.

3. **Photofunia**
   photofunia.com

   Another cool site with plenty of options. The weird thing about this site is that you'll find a lot of graphics that let you swap your face for Santa's, an astronaut's, etc. Weird. Just say no.

Bonus Generator Sites

Here are more of my favorite generator sites. Follow my new discoveries at pinterest.com/nerdybff.

Artist from Photofunia.com

funnywow.com

funphotobox.com

glassgiant.com

loonapix.com

lunapic.com

pho.to

photo505.com

Travel

In This Chapter:

PLUS

TripIt

tripit.com

• •

Almost all of our travel plans these days are confirmed via email, but combing through your inbox to find the name of a hotel when you're in a taxi at the airport is both inconvenient and annoying.

The first time you use **TripIt**, you'll wonder how you ever lived without it. The concept is simple—just forward all your travel confirmations to plans@tripit.com, which is connected to the email address you use to forward. TripIt absorbs your confirmation and makes all the plans available on your mobile device.

Let's say you're planning a trip to Chicago in May. In January, you book the airfare and forward the confirmation. You find the perfect hotel room in April, and you snag a great deal on a rental car the day before you leave. TripIt has been using your forwarded confirmations to organize your trip behind the scenes; and when you head to the airport for your flight to Chicago, you open TripIt on your smartphone and open the trip that the app has named "Chicago, May 2014." Inside, you'll find your flight information, your hotel check-in time and confirmation number, the location of the rental car counter, and even the weather report for your stay. No more digging in your bag to find the confirmation you printed out to tell the taxi driver what hotel you're going to, or searching your email to figure out what time you have to get up to come home.

Using the TripIt Itinerary

1. Once you forward an electronic reservation to plans@tripit.com, TripIt automatically names it by the destination. You can always edit and merge trips online.

2. TripIt shows you the weather forecast for your destination.

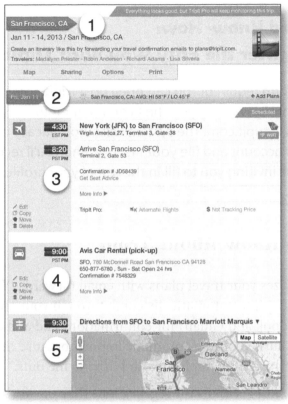

TripIt Itinerary

3. When you forward your confirmation email, TripIt automatically populates all the fields, including flight info and confirmation numbers. If you have TripIt Pro, the system will also monitor for lower rates and better seats.

4. You can forward other reservations as well, and TripIt files them under the same trip so the name of your hotel is easy to find when you get off the plane.

5. TripIt also shows you maps from one destination to another, such as how to get from the airport to your hotel.

Nerd Know-How: Register the Easy Way With TripIt

No form required! You can open up a TripIt account by simply forwarding your first confirmation to plans@tripit.com. The system will automatically create your account and file your first trip, and you'll receive an email inviting you to fill in the rest of your profile.

6 Things to Know About TripIt

1. TripIt organizes your travel plans with email forwards. You can also set up TripIt to automatically comb through your email (Yahoo, Outlook and Gmail) for confirmations and add them to your trips. I turned off the automatic imports because the system kept importing duplicates and driving me nuts.

2. If you use multiple emails for registrations (like one for work and one for home), you can add the additional emails to your account to keep all your reservations in one place.

3. You can also add appointments and other plans into existing reservations.

4. TripIt Pro costs $49 a year and adds all kinds of convenient travel tools. The Price Tracker feature alone once saved me $114—enough for two years of service. TripIt Pro also helps you find alternative flights and monitors airline seating charts for better seats.

5. TripIt lets you access your plans on the go on almost any platform: iOS devices, Android, BlackBerry and Windows Phone.

6. Expense management service Concur bought TripIt a couple of years ago, and if you sign up with both systems (starting at $8

per month for Concur), you can import travel expenses into Concur for easy expense reports.

TripIt Alternative

WorldMate
worldmate.com

WorldMate is a worthy—perhaps superior—TripIt competitor. You don't have to forward your confirmations to WorldMate—it searches automatically. Both services are available on a wide range of mobile platforms, and they run neck-and-neck with their feature lists for the paid versions; but WorldMate's free version includes goodies such as a currency exchange calculator (so you don't have to use a separate one like the **XE Currency** apps). And then there's the price. TripIt Pro is $49 a year, and WorldMate Gold is an app that costs $9.99.

NerdHerd Thumbs Up: WorldMate and TripIt make travel easier

Both Emily Arrowsmith and Sarah Martis love organizing their travel with TripIt. "TripIt requires no management," Sarah says. "You just ensure all of your travel information is sent to the email associated with your account, and it imports everything automatically." Joanne Campbell uses WorldMate to organize maps, itineraries, tickets and more. "It's a great backup, all in one place," Joanne says.

Four Airport Apps and Sites

The travel world is full of apps that help you get from one place to the other with as little hassle as possible. If you travel a lot, apps from providers such as airlines and hotels can be very helpful, as can these tools. Also check out Google Flights, Page 237.

1. **Hipmunk** and 2. **Hopper**
   hipmunk.com and **hopper.com**

   The travel planning site with the adorable mascot, Hipmunk lets you quickly sort travel options by departure or arrival time, and it has an "agony" filter that reveals the flights with the best routes and fewest hassles. NerdHerder Dayne Hodgetts also likes Hopper for its cuteness: "a cute little bunny travel-agent-like advisor for when to buy and fly."

3. **FlightAware**
   flightaware.com

   FlightAware is the first place I go when I want to see if an airport or area is facing delays.

4. **SeatGuru**
   seatguru.com

   Never sit in the worst seat on the plane again. This service shows you seat maps of every plane and offers recommendations for the best spots.

Two Services to Replace Rental Cars

1. **RelayRides**
   relayrides.com

   Instead of heading to the rental counter, you can reserve someone's car while it's parked in his or her driveway. Some smart RelayRides participants will even bring the car to you at the airport to make rentals easier. You can find old Pintos as well as new Ferraris, but I've yet to find a deal that's better than a regular car rental site.

2. **FlightCar**
   flightcar.com

   Parking at the airport for an extended trip? Let someone rent your car while you're gone with FlightCar.

NerdHerd Thumbs Up: FlightAware helps you keep track of loved ones

Joan Teeling knows where her favorite passengers are with FlightAware. She likes that the tracking is live and includes a visual of the plane's location.

Waze

When Apple and Google were fighting over the No. 1 spot for mobile map apps, **Waze** drove up and charmed us all. Like the other two navigation tools, Waze offers turn-by-turn navigation to get you where you want to go; but instead of relying on a database of maps and official traffic reports, Waze lets its members report real-time delays, speed traps, accidents and other road hazards.

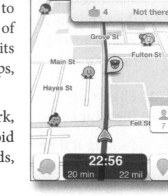

Waze Hazard Alert

When you program in your home and work, the community of users will help you avoid traffic and trouble, such as road hazards, speed traps and traffic jams.

The app will also automatically reroute you when traffic problems significantly impact your arrival time.

Nerd Know-How:
Let Your Peeps Track You with Waze

Do you have any worrywarts in your world who text you 15 times to ask, "Are you on your way? Where are you?" With just a couple of clicks, you can email or text a link to let your worrier track your course and see your ETA. Of course, if you're at the cupcake store and don't want anyone to know, you should turn this feature off.

NerdHerd Thumbs Up:
EVERYONE loves Waze

Five NerdHerders declared Waze their favorite tool. Here's why:

- Elizabeth Armstrong and Lisa Prats like the accurate traffic alerts and other notifications.

- Jeanie Simon says it's user friendly and accurate.

- Robin O. Brown uses Waze to avoid traffic jams and appreciates that Waze reroutes her if necessary.

- And Jeff De Cagna says simply, "Waze is vastly better than any other navigation app . . . IT TOTALLY ROCKS!"

Waze encourages chattiness and helpfulness with a point system, plus it connects with your social networks to let you and your friends keep tabs on one another. Now that it's part of the Google empire, look for even more integrations and connections, including being pre-installed on some Android devices.

Waze also helps you find the lowest prices on gas in your area, with data available from other members as well as Yelp and Foursquare. And the service lets you collect coupons and specials from participating merchants during your travels, although these pop-ups get annoying while you're driving.

Waze Changing Route

5 Things to Know About Waze

1. Waze is a turn-by-turn navigation app that gives you real-time updates from fellow drivers on your route.

2. You can change the voice (Elvis is my favorite), but only the basic voices pronounce the street names.

3. Waze has voice control options so you can give hands-free reports, but the sensor is very annoying. I turned it off because I kept accidentally brushing the phone and hearing, "How can I help?" over and over.

4. One of the most useful features allows you to send a link to your contacts so they can track you on your route.

5. Although things have improved with the help of Google Maps, Waze still relies on other users to help map areas and find routes. I've ended up taking the long way around several times because of inaccurate maps.

Nerd Know-How: Take the Back Road

As a commuter, you're going to love how Waze sees traffic trouble down the road and routes you through the back roads to avoid the mess. But the people in those back-road neighborhoods are not happy. Waze is making whole neighborhoods angry as it routes scores of commuters through formerly quiet neighborhoods during rush hours.

Waze Alternatives

- **Moovit**
  moovitapp.com

  If you're looking for a Waze-type guide for public transportation, **Moovit** is an international resource of real-time updates from fellow passengers. Maps are now available for major cities worldwide.

- **AXSmap**
  axsmap.com

  NerdHerder Joan Eisenstodt gives a thumbs up to AXSmap, which she calls "Yelp for people with disabilities." The site lets people share locations and routes that are accessible. Joan says she uses it to "go places on my scooter and know I'll get in."

NerdHerd Thumbs Up:
Local travel apps come in handy

Many cities do a great job of sharing local transportation updates in custom apps. NerdHerder Dianne Richards uses MTA BusTime (bustime.mta.info) to see when the NYC buses are due. "I know if I've just missed the bus or it's just running late."

Five Alarm Clock Apps

Waze and TripIt can get you to where you're going on time, but only if you get out of bed. These alarm apps are great on the road and at home.

1. **Sleep Time**
   azumio.com/apps/sleep-time

   This alarm is my favorite. You sleep with your phone next to you on the bed and it monitors your sleep cycle. When your alarm goes off, the app will gently wake you during a lighter sleep cycle so you aren't jolted from a deep sleep.

2. **Wakie**
   wakie.com

   Wakie is a little weird—OK, maybe even creepy. This alarm app connects its users so that strangers give you your wake-up call. No one sees anyone else's phone number, but still. Weird. If no one is around to call you, it defaults to a regular alarm.

3. **SpinMe**
   spinmealarm.com

   This may be too annoying to actually use, but if you really have trouble waking up in the morning, SpinMe might be the answer. It makes you wake up and shimmy around before it turns off.

4. **Nightstand**

Karen Clark from My Business Presence recommends the Nightstand app from Kinsington (in the iTunes App Store). She uses it on the road as an easy-to-read clock for hotel nightstands. Plus, Karen says, "I'm a speaker, and I bring it on stage with me to keep track of the time. It's easy to see from a distance whether it's on a table or the floor."

5. **Carrot**
meetcarrot.com/alarm

All the Carrot apps are mean-girl motivators. The Fit app calls its workout "7 Minutes of Hell" and promises encouragement and "threats of bodily harm." One of the exercises suggests you imagine "punching Justin Bieber in his pretty face." The Hunger app keeps you from eating too much by using social shaming as it counts your calories.

And as for the Carrot Alarm, don't dare to try to sleep late— that's all I have to say.

NerdHerd Thumbs Up:
Focus@Will helps you, well, focus

Sheri Fitts (from the cleverly titled ShoeFitts Marketing) says, "I love, love, love Focus@Will." The site and apps offer a subscription for music to work by that promotes alpha brain waves and helps you concentrate.

Outsource

· ·

In This Chapter:

PLUS

Fancy Hands

fancyhands.com

These days am on the road more than half of every month. I was lugging around a briefcase that was awesome in airport security lanes because all I had to do was unzip it rather than pull out the computer. But the dang thing weighed about 90 pounds, or so it seemed when I slung it over my shoulder trip after trip.

To save my shoulders, I had to find a replacement—an attractive, airport-friendly, professional bag with wheels—in a nerd-friendly color! Every time I picked up my old briefcase to travel, I thought about the elusive bag. I would search occasionally, but it was just taking too long to find the perfect one. So I went on abusing my back with the old bag for months.

Then I discovered **Fancy Hands,** a completely nifty site that takes tiny tasks off your plate for $5 to $6 per request or less. Its packages start at $30 per month for up to five tasks, and they roll over. I'm at the 15-task level.

One of the first tasks I sent was to find me the perfect bag; and within three days, I had a link to an orange, checkpoint-friendly, wheeled tote—on sale even. Fancy Hands helps me set appointments, track down lost mail, create cool graphics, research tech tools—you name it—all kinds of little 20-minute tasks that can take me out of work mode and make me lose more time.

Using Fancy Hands

Once you sign up for a Fancy Hands subscription, you can submit tasks a number of ways. I usually send an email, but you can also call the tasks in or enter them on the website, where your Dashboard tracks all your tasks and gives you a snapshot of the work Fancy Hands has done for you. It also gives you little trophies for achieving time-saving goals.

Outsource

When you submit your task on the site, you can narrow it down to specific areas, such as admin or shopping. It's generally easier to just fire off an email and let the system categorize it for you.

Fancy Hands is FAST! I've submitted tasks on weekends and holidays, and almost all of them are completed and back to me within the hour. It doesn't promise to make any type of deadline, but you can indicate that a task is time-sensitive when you send it in.

Fancy Hands
Status

Tasks I've Assigned to Fancy Hands:

- Set a vet appointment for my kittens.

- Create a spreadsheet from business cards.

- Get high-res logos for tech tools I write about.

- Coordinate a meeting with a client.

- Retype text from cranky PDFs into a Word doc.

- Research what we should do on vacation in Nashville.

- Grab a list of sponsor names from a website so I can create custom graphics for an engagement.

- Find the best printer at the best price during the Black Friday shopping holiday.

- Check the website URLs for tools in my book.

- Locate the perfect briefcase.

- Find replacement doohickeys for said briefcase when they pop off.

Get a great room
06/26 at 11:51 AM

How did we do?

Please call the following hotel and beg them to give me the very best room with the very best possible internet signal since I'll be writing my third book during my stay. The book will be all about technology, so I'll be surfing nonstop and need a great wifi signal. THANKS!

http://screencast.com/t/vvxtlhuxu5q

July 18-28 Confirmation # A7BT2G

Fancy Hands Request

Colleen T.

3 weeks ago

Hello Elizabeth,
They said that all the rooms have the same strong wifi signal. Thank you for using Fancy Hands!

Sincerely,
Colleen T.

Fancy Hands Response

Fancy Hands Integrations

Fancy Hands has connections that help simplify your workflows.

- **Evernote** (Page 14)
  Fancy Hands can save every task and the results into an Evernote Notebook so you can look things up wherever you are.

- **Conference Calling**
  You can use one of your tasks to schedule a conference call inside the Fancy Hands system. Just put in your date and time as well as the emails of the attendees. Fancy Hands will set up the call (dial-in number and everything) and even dial out to the participants to join the event.

- **Project Management**
Fancy Hands connects with Basecamp, Asana and Trello (Page 44) so you can track your tasks and check off your to-dos in your project management system of choice.

- **Shopping**
Like the Fetch app (Page 187), Fancy Hands can locate products and make authorized purchases on your behalf.

Nerd Know-How: Transcribe Business Cards with Fancy Hands

You can find a whole bunch of business card apps and readers, such as **CamCard** (camcard.com) and Evernote's service (Page 20). But, in my humble opinion, they all suck. When you have to enter a whole stack of cards, you can use these tools to snap a picture, but then you have to verify all the info and accept the data before moving on. It's almost easier to just type them into a spreadsheet.

But it's even easier to have someone else type them into a spreadsheet. After every event, I neatly spread the business cards over the bedspread in my hotel room. Then I snap pictures of the cards (two cards per pic). My iPhone lets me select images for a public photo stream, so I dump all the cards into iCloud and send the link off to Fancy Hands. In less than an hour, I have the completed spreadsheet to upload into my MailChimp (Page 123) newsletter list.

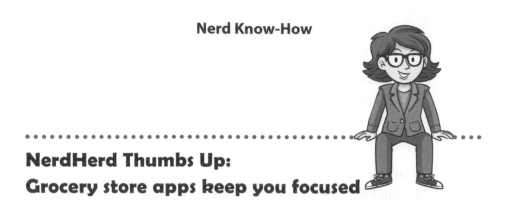

Nerd Know-How

NerdHerd Thumbs Up:
Grocery store apps keep you focused

Speaking of tools that help you stay on track, NerdHerder Susan Klemmer uses the Wegmans App (wegmans.com/mobile) to quickly find items on her shopping list in her grocery store. "They keep moving stuff in my Wegmans, and I usually shop there on my lunch hour," Susan says. "I don't have time to wander, and when I do, I spend too much!"

6 Things to Know About Fancy Hands

1. Fancy Hands employs a stable of U.S.-based virtual assistants who take annoying little tasks off your list so you can concentrate on getting work done.

2. It used to be pretty relaxed about what a task was, but now it strictly limits the work to about 20 minutes. If you send a project that might take longer than that, Fancy Hands may send you back an email to authorize additional tasks to fulfill the project.

3. You can start a task with an email, a call or a visit to the app or website.

4. It can integrate your tasks with Basecamp (Page 48), your Google Calendar (Page 225) and more.

5. You can provide a credit card number, and your assistant can make purchases on your behalf.

6. When I first started using Fancy Hands assistants, I had them call customers for testimonials and other things. I found that the quality of the assistants varied widely, and I couldn't count on them to be on the front lines of customer service.

Five Apps that Do Things for You

Fancy Hands is not the only way to get out of tasks and errands. These apps put people and technology at your disposal to get stuff done.

1. **Fetch**
   buywithfetch.com

   Let's pretend you're on the run and realize you need to buy a new pair of nerd socks (this happens to me a lot). A new app called Fetch hooks you up with a personal shopper who searches for the items you seek and comes back with pricing or just buys it for you. You can hook up your Amazon Prime account so you get free shipping, or it keeps your credit card on file to use elsewhere.

   I tried it out with a pair of nerdy socks. I had just purchased a dozen for $7.99 each. I asked Fetch to find the best price on the same pair. Within 3 minutes, my personal shopper wrote back a happy message that she had found a pair and a coupon, so the price would only be $12 and change.

   I wrote back, "Hmmm . . . I just bought it 10 minutes ago for $7.99 including shipping." Things got quiet for a minute, and then I got an email from the owner of Fetch, explaining that my Amazon Prime account takes a few minutes to appear, and that's why I didn't get the best price yet.

   Although my personal shopper took a while to find the great pricing, you'll appreciate the interface and the ease. And the fact that the founder wrote me back immediately speaks volumes for the customer service.

2. **Assistant.to**
   trybetty.com

   OK, this meeting scheduling tool is very new, and perhaps it won't make it. But it has a great concept. Once you set up an account with Assistant.to, a bar appears on the bottom of your Gmail compose page. From there, you can choose timeframes from up to three dates to insert into your email automatically. Your meeting partner then just clicks on the preferred time, and the event is added to both of your calendars. I had trouble with the time zones for one call, but it seems to have fixed that issue.

3. **Path Talk**
   path.com/talk

   Before it was purchased by Path, TalkTo was an amazing stand-alone app. TalkTo let you text any company in the U.S. or Canada and get a response within 5 minutes. You could write to all the local Target stores in your area to see if anyone has a red, junior-size sleeping bag that your kid just informed you he would need for a camping trip this weekend.

   But Path bought it, and the service is now integrated into the Path Talk interface. I'm not saying this is a bad thing, but now you'll have to sign up for a Path account and work within its confines. We'll see how it all works out.

4. **FileThis**
   filethis.com

   I don't know about your early spring, but things can get a little prickly around our house when my husband does our taxes. One of the sticking points was always the gathering of all the statements. He was always waiting on me to get my credit card and bank paperwork into his hands.

   FileThis has eased the tension. The service automatically fetches your bank statements, credit card paperwork and more.

I set up a Dropbox folder for all the PDFs, and my husband just opens the folder during tax time and grabs what he needs without bugging me. Heaven.

5. **Shoeboxed**
   shoeboxed.com

   How many wrinkled, stained, faded receipts do you have in your desk right now? You know you need to record them somewhere, but it's such a pain that you probably just let them pile up and make you feel guilty.

   Shoeboxed is a service that lets you snap a picture of something you need transcribed, or, even better, lets you physically send stuff to someone else who will unwrinkle and decipher the hard-to-read contents to extract the important info.

   It's been around for quite some time, and I used to have a yearly subscription. At its lowest paid level, about a hundred bucks a year will let you send in up to 50 documents a month, including things such as business cards, documents and receipts. It'll scan and categorize everything for you and provide you a beautiful portal where you can export the organized information for expense reports, taxes, contact management and more.

NerdHerd Thumbs Up:
Nike gets you going

Susan Patereau is a REALTOR® on the go. No, really. She uses Nike+ Running (nike.com) to keep track of her running activity and log her routes.

Fiverr

fiverr.com

Need to build a new website? Or clean up an old database? Or revamp your marketing material? Help is on the way!

When I need something done, my first thought is always **Fiverr**. Fiverr is a marketplace of literally thousands of people who do all kinds of stuff—for $5.

Five bucks. Yes, indeed. The site presents the engagements in an attractive format and gives you plenty of ways to search for the right freelancer.

Sample Fiverr Gigs

You'll be amazed at the variety of freelance projects you can get for five bucks, such as:

- Create a simple banner ad.
- Write a customized limerick.
- Make a tough decision.
- Tweet your message to thousands of followers.
- Record a voiceover in a native British accent.
- Add music to your video.
- Send your child a personalized letter from Santa Claus.
- Create a QR Code.

And on, and on and on. Hilarious and fun!

The first time I used Fiverr, I spent about $100 trying things out; and I was very pleasantly surprised with the results. I ended up with several videos that range from "eh" to "WOW!"—All for $5!

Since then I've spent hundreds on little projects, everything from a jingle for Your Nerdy Best Friend to promo videos from the Posh English Lady to expertise to fix my WordPress website.

I've had very mixed results with my attempts to get someone to design a T-shirt for me and to design a logo, even though I hired five people at a time in hopes of finding one winner. I also hired several Fiverrs to design the cartoon nerds in this book. After my NerdHerd members decided on the winning drawing, I hired the artist to produce a bunch of poses.

Here is a sample of the little cartoon Beths. Although the second one is probably the closest likeness to me, in my mind, I look more like the last one.

Cartoon Beths

NerdHerd Thumbs Up:
My personal trainer loves Fiverr

Gianna Caruso is the best personal trainer in the universe (despite the fact that I can't seem to lose a pound even when I work out with her). Sometimes when I'm trying to distract her from kicking my nerdy little rear in a workout, I tell her about cool tech tools. That's how she fell in love with Fiverr, which helps her with small projects for her career development and just for fun.

6 Things to Know About Fiverr

1. Fiverr is a marketplace of freelancers and a great resource for any small business that needs to outsource projects.

2. If you can't find a gig you want, you can write a description of your project and request bids. This option is a little hard to find, though. Look under your Shopping tab or way down in teeny print at the bottom.

3. It's smart to choose three to five designers for the same project to see which one gives you a better product. You're still not out very much money, but you'll get a variety of results that you can build on.

4. Fiverr gigs will often cost you more than five bucks because of the add-ons, plus they recently added an extra service fee, so even the $5 gigs are $5.50. You may pay extra for a rush job or for the addition of color or a background to a graphic. You're

still paying very little for someone's hard work, so the upgrades are easily worth it.

5. Good ratings are like gold to the freelancers, and I once had an argument with a provider about a thumbs down I had given. I was dissatisfied with the work, but the guy kept writing and complaining that my negative review was hurting him. I caved and gave him a better rating, but I've heard a couple of similar stories. Stay strong.

6. The words "Fiverr®," "Gig®" and a bunch of other stuff are trademarked. Fiverr wants me to use the little symbols whenever I mention them. That's kind of a pain, so let's pretend I did that, OK?

Fiverr Alternatives

Fiverr has many, many imitators with names such as **Fourer** and **Twentyville**. But Fiverr is the leader and the best. But you might like **SEO-Clerks**, a marketplace specifically for SEO services with prices that range from $1 to $999.

Nerd Know-How: Commission Custom Freelance Projects

The best way to work with Fiverr is to take it for what it is—a marketplace of people who sell certain goods and services. When I am looking for a graphic, I peruse what they're offering rather than try to get them to conform to what I'm thinking. Fiverr has an area where you can request a gig, but you're limited in words; and I'm guessing that getting exactly what you want will take longer than if you used a service-for-hire platform such as Elance (Page 196).

Elance

elance.com

Although Fiverr (Page 192) is awesome, you're not always going to get away with a $5 project to advance your business. For larger projects, you can find any number of freelancer marketplaces; and on each site, you can find thousands and thousands of proven experts who can help you with every imaginable task. I think of them as Craigslist on steroids where you can find potential contractors, evaluate their ratings, keep track of their work and control the payment.

When I need to outsource a large project, I head to **Elance**. You describe your project and set the parameters: your budget, your timeline, your hopes and dreams for a successful project. Then you open your project for bids to the marketplace. To find the right person, you might want to search the providers and invite your favorites to bid. If you're commissioning an illustration, for example, hop around in their portfolios to find a designer with a style you like.

Elance Freelancers

You'll probably get from five to 50 proposals; and as they come in, you can add more info to the project description, correspond with the individual bidders, eliminate the yucky ones and rank your top choices. The providers on these sites will have reviews, recommendations and examples—check it all out to make sure you find the right person.

Once you declare a winner on Elance, the site serves as a super-efficient project management tool. You and your new contractor agree on the project terms. On larger projects, you can divide up payments with the milestones. As you work, the system acts like your own Basecamp site (Page 48). Every email you send is cataloged in the system. Every file you exchange is kept in the workroom. Every milestone is tracked. The system even has communication tools such as live chat and screensharing (from Join.me, Page 63) built in. Elance holds the funds in escrow until you release them, so you stay in charge of the money.

6 Things to Know About
Elance and Freelancing Sites

1. On Elance you'll find every possible freelancer to support your business, from tech help to marketing expertise to personal assistants.

2. Elance just merged with a major competitor, ODesk, so it's bigger and stronger than ever.

3. It's kind of a chore to find the right freelancer. Plan on taking several hours to narrow down your top choices. Don't be afraid to write and ask for clarification. Projects work best if everyone is on the same page from the beginning.

4. Overall my experience on Elance has been positive, but I've had a few stinkers. Be clear in your instructions and needs, and give feedback freely. You can cancel a project and get a refund if you're not happy, but you may waste time and money getting to the point where you call it quits.

5. Once you find a freelancer you like, you can create jobs just for her without opening up to other bidders.

6. You'll find freelancers from every country on Elance. You can filter for providers in a certain area, within a given price range, with a specific ratings level and more.

Elance Alternatives

- **99designs**
  99designs.com

  Let's say your organization has a big event every year, and you're looking for a logo that would brand the conference series. You could hire your favorite graphic designer to come up with 10 to 20 ideas for several hundred to several thousand dollars. Or you could hold a logo design contest on a crowdsourcing site for $299+ to have dozens of designers come up with ideas that you could narrow down to your top choices and share with your potential attendees for a vote.

  I adore these kinds of contests, both for finding the perfect logo and for strengthening your community. Rather than getting one expert's ideas for your logo, you get ideas from many. I had more than 100 variations of my present logo before I picked the best one. As the contest continues, you can give feedback to your top contenders to get them to refine and rework the colors and designs to help bring your vision to life. 99designs also helps you find designers for book covers, T-shirt designs and much more.

Many freelancers hate these kinds of sites. I once received a very long, very thorough "shame on you" email from a designer friend. Sites like these, she said, devalue the work that a professional freelancer does. The design sites are rife with copyright infringement issues. The low prices exploit unknown workforces. And they don't produce quality, well-thought-out work.

I have worked with many freelancers from these sites, and I always felt like they thought our partnership was valuable to their businesses. So I'm all for them, although I make it a point to consider all bids, not just the cheapest. The choice is yours about whether you want to use these sites to take tasks off your to-do lists.

Your Nerdy Best Friend Logo Contest

- **Freelancer.com**

This major competitor now offers a variety of services to help you find the perfect freelancer. You can post a project or a contest as with 99designs.

- **Ziptask**
  ziptask.com

Ziptask says it'll help guide you in your search for and use of a freelancer, even at its most basic levels. For large projects, you can hire a Ziptask project management team to work with you to develop and execute your projects.

Nerd Know-How:
Hold a Design Contest with 99designs

Book covers can cost upwards of $5,000, but design contests on 99designs start at a few hundred dollars. I bought the $799 Gold level, and I ended up with 281 designs from dozens of talented designers. After a little help from almost 600 of my newsletter readers and social media followers, I narrowed it down to my top four designers and asked them to iron out the last little details.

The competition came down to two awesome options:

99designs Book Cover Options

Either one would have been amazing, but obviously you know which ultimately prevailed.

Three Tools to Build a Blog

Small business folks often seek professionals to build major projects like new websites or a blog. If you're a do-it-yourself nerd, give these blog builders a try.

1. **WordPress**
   wordpress.com

   WordPress sites have come a long way. When the company opened its doors in 2003, it offered simple sites that allowed you to write and share snippets of your life online. As of January 2015, WordPress claims it is the basis for more than 60 million websites.

   Starting a WordPress blog or website is easy, for both personal and business use. For a free hosted site with a URL such as nerdybestfriend.wordpress.com, simply create an account and pick a name at WordPress.com. There, you can also purchase various upgrades, including a custom URL if you want your blog or site to live at nerdybestfriend.com. If you want total control—including a custom URL, a wide variety of plug-ins and the capability to sell your own advertising—you can download the free WordPress software from WordPress.org; but you must arrange and pay for hosting of the site.

   The next step in building your site with WordPress is choosing a theme, and here's where the magic begins. You can choose from thousands of free themes, or for less than $100, you can buy an easy-to-install framework for a full site, complete with the embedded blog for dynamic content, or not. I find great templates from Envato (Page 129) and **WooThemes** (woothemes.com). My assistant, Molly, loves **Elegant Themes** (elegantthemes.com). You can further personalize your site with any of the thousands of plug-ins and widgets to do everything from embed video to automatically tweet your posts to Twitter to install a carousel-type photo gallery.

2. Tumblr
tumblr.com

The microblogging site Tumblr has become a blog platform to be reckoned with. It's free and easy to create a new site, and users find Tumblr a great way to find and share updates from their favorite information curators. In January 2015, Tumblr added long-form blogging capability that will transform the homepage views from looking like snippets of info to a wordier (and more traditional) standard.

3. Medium
medium.com

There's something calming about the white background and black words of Medium, a new blogging platform from the founder of Twitter. There are no themes, no blinking boxes, no busy columns. Medium has text and pictures and words and ideas. You write your piece, and the world can respond—even to a very specific area of your post. You can make collections of other content on your pages, and the most popular posts end up on the front page. Medium is simple, stark, beautiful and purposeful; and it seamlessly integrates into your social media world.

Another breakthrough for Medium: Politicians, including President Barack Obama, are starting to use Medium for transcripts of speeches, policy statements, proposed budgets and more.

Nerd Know-How:
Make Your Website Mobile Friendly

Many people turn WordPress blogs into business websites or create their own using low-cost services such as **Wix** (wix.com) and **Squarespace** (squarespace.com). But your site will suck unless it's mobile friendly. Google Search recently started penalizing sites that didn't have a mobile version. You might use a platform like **Strikingly** (strikingly.com), which helps you create a mobile-friendly site from the get-go rather than having to convert a standard site into something that looks good on the go.

Guess who told me he loves Strikingly? THE Seth Godin—best-selling author of every essential book you need to read! Seth told me, "Here's a site that's both easy to use and beautiful. Try as you might, you won't mess it up! If you need a responsive website, this is a fine place to start."

Google

In This Chapter:

PLUS

Gmail

· ·

Oh boy. What can I say about Gmail—or rather, what *can't* I say about Gmail? In my humble opinion, Gmail is the strongest tool in my Google toolbox, followed closely by Calendar (Page 225). I could write a whole book about Gmail functions, integrations and tips, but I'll try to concentrate on the most useful features that will help you take control of your email.

Nerd Know-How: Should You Trust Google?

Love it or hate it, the giant geekdom that is Google integrates incredibly tightly into our modern technological world. Even if you don't have a Google account, you probably watch cat videos on YouTube, get directions to Uncle Joe's house from Google Maps and search for cupcake recipes via Google Search. Google is almost impossible to avoid.

Some people worry about the power that Google has over our data and privacy; but if you can get past that, you can find an almost infinite treasure trove of free tech tools that can organize and enhance your life, both at home and at work.

Use Gmail Anywhere

One of the best benefits of Gmail is the ability to take it with you wherever you go. Gmail lives in the cloud, so you can access it from any browser or device. I can start composing an email on my computer and finish it on my phone. When I clean out my inbox on my iPad, everything syncs. It just works. And it's awesome.

Connect Everything to Gmail

Like Dropbox (Page 2), Gmail is one of the first integrations that third-party apps create to expand their capabilities. I don't think I could find a complete list of plug-ins, add-ons, apps and extensions—they're just everywhere. Most of them require permission to connect, and you can find a list of everything you've authorized in your Google Account settings under Security (Page 236).

Gmail Add-Ons

- **Boomerang**
  boomeranggmail.com

  Use Boomerang to schedule an email to pop back into your inbox at a certain time. This helps you remember to follow up with clients, write back to your mom and more.

- **Unroll.me**

  If your Gmail inbox (or Yahoo! or AOL or more) overflows with subscriptions, promotions and just plain old junk, Unroll.me can help. It analyzes and categorizes your email, making it darn easy to unsubscribe or organize. You can gather all the regular updates you get into one digest and get rid of all the rest.

  My assistant, Molly, loves to organize her wanted-but-not-needed email with Unroll.me. "I keep one digest for just coupons and groups and stuff!"

- **Cirrus Insight**
  cirrusinsight.com

  I used to pay $5 a month for the basic level of Salesforce (Page 59) so I could keep track of conversations without having to save everything in my inbox. But it was a pain to go back and forth from Gmail to Salesforce to log information. Cirrus Insight was $19 a month to connect my Gmail to Salesforce with a menu to the right of the inbox. Every time someone sent me a note, I entered the contact info into Salesforce without leaving Gmail and saved all the correspondence with a click.

  An additional handy feature is a little creepy—Cirrus Insight tracks outgoing mail and lets users know when and where it's opened. An additional tool called **Yesware** (yesware.com) has tracking as well with a free version.

- **Discoverly**
  discover.ly

  Wouldn't it be helpful to see critical info about your contacts without having to leave your inbox? Discoverly pulls in social media profiles and other info into a panel right near your contact's name as you're corresponding. You also get bonus info when you visit your social media sites, like the box that shows up below my buddy Bruce Turkel's Twitter profile.

Bruce Turkel's Twitter Profile with Discoverly

Get All Your Email Through Gmail

As I've traveled through life, I've picked up quite a few email addresses. Gmail lets me pull all the accounts into one system to send and receive everything in one place. Warning: Every time I've added emails, the process has taken me much longer than I think it should because of all the little options and steps and settings.

1. To send and receive emails from other accounts, you have to take several steps. First, to receive, you want to set up a POP3 mail account under Settings >> Accounts and Import.

Check mail from other accounts (using POP3): Learn more	**beth@askbethz.com** Last checked: 1 minute ago. View history Check mail now
	beth@avenuez.net Last checked: 2 minutes ago. View history Check mail now
	beth@yournerdybestfriend.com Last checked: 3 minutes ago. View history Check mail now
	bziesenis@avenuez.net Last checked: 3 minutes ago. View history Check mail now
	① Add a POP3 mail account you own
Using Gmail for work?	Companies can power their email with Gmail for businesses.
Grant access to your account: (Allow others to read and send mail on your behalf) Learn more	Add another account ② ○ **Mark conversation as read when opened by others** ◉ **Leave conversation unread when opened by others**
Add additional storage:	You are currently using 1.38 GB (9%) of your 15 GB. Need more space? Purchase additional storage

Add POP3 Email in Gmail

2. From here you can also give access to someone else to check your mail. I have found this handy for my assistants. They can check mail and answer it as themselves on my behalf.

Add a mail account you own

Enter the mail settings for info@yournerdybestfriend.com. Learn more

Email address: **info@yournerdybestfriend.com**
1   Username: info
    Password:
2   POP Server: mail.yournerdybestfriend.com   Port: 110
    ☐ Leave a copy of retrieved message on the server. Learn more
    ☐ Always use a secure connection (SSL) when retrieving mail. Learn more
3   ☐ Label incoming messages: info@yournerdybestfriend.com
    ☐ Archive incoming messages (Skip the Inbox)

Cancel   « Back   Add Account »

Adding an Email Account

3. A dialog box opens to add your email. Here's where the system starts to get very picky. To find all the settings for your email, look for a manual configuration info box somewhere with your host. It should tell you the mysterious settings for sending (outgoing) and receiving (incoming) mail.

**Secure SSL/TLS Settings
(Recommended)**

Username: info@yournerdybestfriend.com

Password: *Use the email account's password.*

**Incoming
Server:**   IMAP Port: 993
                 POP3 Port: 995

**Outgoing
Server:**   SMTP Port: 465

Authentication is required for IMAP, POP3, and SMTP.

Manual Email Configuration

4. Enter your incoming server web address and the port.

5. You can now choose whether you want Gmail to leave a duplicate copy of the emails on your server (so they can be accessed with a service such as **web2mail.com** with just your username and password). Another helpful option here is to automatically create a label in Gmail so these emails stand out.

Once you have your email set up, you should note that the external emails will not come in immediately. Gmail checks every few minutes. When I'm desperately waiting for an email from something (like a link to a movie I just created for a session that begins in 2 minutes), I always use my Gmail address to receive the email instantly instead of ones I've added that have to go through an external server.

Fetching Alternate Emails in Gmail

Nerd Know-How: Control Spam with Gmail

The Gmail spam filter is one of the best I've ever seen, and it even works on the emails you import from other services.

Nerd Know-How

After you set up receiving emails from other accounts, you still need to add the ability to send emails from the original accounts. Otherwise your replies will come through your Gmail account.

1. You want to uncheck the alias option so that your emails are sent from the right account.

Treat as an Alias Option

2. You can also choose whether you want to reply to emails with a different email address, such as answering a generic email like info@yournerdybestfriend.com with a more personal address like **beth@yournerdybestfriend.com**.

Choosing the SMTP Server and Port

The next step is also picky. Make sure you refer to your manual configuration information to choose the right SMTP server and port. I've also had trouble with the username field. Just triple check.

Your mail configuration should recommend your secured connection options. My host asks me to choose SSL. I listen to my host.

Once you set things up, send yourself some test messages. I've never done it right the first time.

Nerd Know-How: Get More from Gmail Labs

Dig under the hood of your Gmail Settings (just click on the little gear icon), and you'll find a super-secret treasure trove of extras called Labs. Labs are experimental add-ons for Gmail, and they may disappear or break at any time (though I've never really had any problems). You have all kinds of cool features to play with, including:

1. A way to create canned responses for an email that you have to rewrite a dozen times a week.

2. The ability to "unsend" an email if you're writing your boss when you're angry or an ex after a night of margaritas. Hey, it happens.

3. A tool that verifies certain senders so you don't fall for a spam email that looks like it came from your bank.

Integrate with Other Google Functions Through Gmail

Google makes it (fairly) easy for its services to work together. If it sees a time and date in an email, it will link directly to your Google Calendar (Page 225). You can turn an email into a **Google Task** with a click. And you can start a **Google+ Hangout** (Page 71) from your contacts list.

5 Things to Know About Gmail

1. Gmail is a cloud-based email system from the powerhouse that is Google.

2. You get a Gmail address when you register with Google, but you can also import your other email addresses into the reader. Each email address can have its own signature, and you can choose which email to reply from no matter the source of the email.

3. Gmail's spam filter helps keep your inbox clean, and its classification system for promotions, updates, important emails and more helps keep you organized.

4. About a kabillion third-party apps integrate with Gmail to make it better.

5. Google works very hard to make email management better and better. The day before I finished this chapter, Google released a new tool called **Inbox**, which makes it easier to organize your inbox and get things done faster and easier. And because the system analyzes your email, you'll see quick links to track packages when you get a postal mailing confirmation, or check your travel schedule when it sees a flight registration. Gmail is also working closer with Google Calendar (Page 225). If you receive a flight confirmation via Gmail, chances are it'll show up in Calendar without any work on your end (kinda presumptuous, isn't it?).

Nerd Know-How:
Check Email and Calendar in One App

In early 2015, Microsoft released a powerful new email app that brings together two essential business tools: your email and your schedule. The **Outlook** app (microsoft.com/en-us/outlook-com/mobile) adds popular email management features such as left/right swiping for email triage, but the addition of calendar access is truly genius. You can flip back and forth to your schedule rather than having to stop and check meeting times on a different app. The system also lets you insert alternative times for meetings into your email.

Believe it or not, Microsoft made it easy with this app to bring in your Gmail accounts and other emails, so you don't have to check multiple sites, though you should know that if you've set up multiple emails through Gmail, you will probably be limited to sending emails from your main Gmail account.

Four Video Email Tools

Now that you've gotten your inbox under control, how can you help your recipients find your message in their piles of emails? Video email can help.

1. **Eyejot**
   eyejot.com

   With thousands of emails drowning inboxes every week, we need to do what we can to get people to notice our notes and to get our messages across. Eyejot is video email that you can create from your computer or mobile device. Not only is it a personal touch for your recipients, the graphics and video link will stand out in a mailbox.

   Eyejot has a robust free version, but I think the $100 a year version is worth it for businesses because you can personalize the template and make the format work for calls to action and more.

2. **BombBomb**
   bombbomb.com

   A reader wrote me about BombBomb. I'm not wild about the name of this tool, but I guess "Eyejot" isn't a wonderful name either. BombBomb's pricing is set up like an email newsletter, where you pay by the number of contacts in your account (starting at $25 a month). It has professional templates to help you frame your message, with special emphasis for real estate and ministry industries.

3. **MailVU**
mailvu.com

Starting at $2.50 a month, you get a basic video email service with handy features such as a self-destruct time limit and a button for your website to let people record testimonials (at the $40 a month level). I also like its option for a video contest—perhaps we can ask for your favorite tools and do a video contest ourselves!

4. **Talk Fusion**
talkfusion.com

I don't do video very often because I rarely bother getting out of my PJs when I work from home, but if you're REALLY into this video stuff, you might consider Talk Fusion. It does more than just video emails, adding video newsletters, blogs, conferencing and more into the mix (starting at the second-highest tier). The smallest package is $125 a year.

NerdHerd Thumbs Up: Super nerdy stuff for Android devices

My NerdHerd friend Eric Witmayer always comes up with the nerdiest tools around. He recommends a tool called Towelroot (towelroot.org) to get into the inner workings of your Android device to make it truly personalized.

YouTube
youtube.com

● ●

YouTube reached its 10th birthday in 2015, but it's kind of hard to remember a time when it wasn't around. The statistics are staggering: Every month more than 1 billion unique users visit YouTube and watch more than 6 billion hours of video. Every minute, users upload more than 100 hours of video. The site makes bucket loads of money for Google with ad revenue. YouTube stars appear out of nowhere, uploading videos from their basements and becoming viral sensations.

YouTube is the world's second-largest search engine (behind you-know-what), and maintaining a hearty YouTube channel is a great way for businesses to stand out. For a researcher or presenter, YouTube is also a perfect resource.

YouTube Video Tools

One of the super-secret YouTube features is the ability to edit the heck out of your videos inside the site itself. When you hit the button to

YouTube Video Editor

edit a video, you can change not only the name and tags but also the video itself.

Enhancements

1. Apply quick fixes such as stabilization and auto-fix presets to clean up a video in a flash.

2. The Filters tab lets you apply color tones over your video.

3. Worried about lawsuits? The Special Effects tab will attempt to blur the faces of everyone in your video.

4. If you're really ambitious, you can combine multiple videos, change audio and do all kinds of fancy things in the full YouTube Video Editor.

Nerd Know-How: Add Background Music to Your Videos

The Audio tab reveals thousands of royalty-free songs you can use as background music for your video. Just choose one and set the volume level to play over your video.

Annotations

Another awesome way to add a little something extra to your YouTube videos is with the Annotations feature. Here's where you can add screen pop-ups that tell your audience about other videos they might like and more. You can program when and where each annotation will pop up.

The digital elephant in the room is that everyone hates pop-ups, right? Why would we put them on our own videos? Well, if you use them correctly and don't get too obnoxious, pop-ups can help your viewers find more information they might want and need (or maybe you can make cute facts come up—like VH1 Pop Up Videos. I can watch those for hours!). You can also create "cards," cute little annotations that look a little more modern than traditional pop-ups.

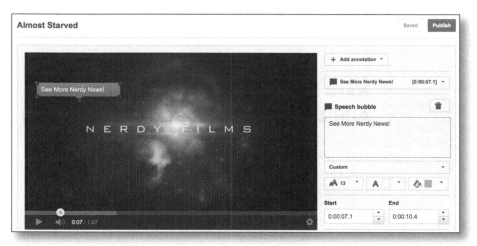

YouTube Annotations

Branding

One of the reasons that some businesses may shy away from developing a YouTube Channel is that our home-baked videos look, well, home baked. They lack that fancy branding and cool touch of a professionally produced video. But in 2014, YouTube snuck in some amazing branding tools to help anyone's YouTube video look more polished.

The secret branding sauce is a little hard to find. Look for it under Channel options in InVideo Programming. There you'll find options to add a watermark and to promote additional videos automatically.

Captioning and Transcribing

YouTube can automatically add captions to your videos, but, ummm, well, it's not a one-button fix. When I checked the captions on one of my videos, I couldn't believe how inaccurate they were. "Your Nerdy Best Friend here . . . Beth Z" was translated as "unity best friend here betsy," and it went downhill from there. Perhaps I speak too quickly or I just have too much music in my voice. Whatever the reason, I was grateful that the service gives me the ability to manually edit all the captions and republish the video.

YouTube Captioning

5 Things to Know About YouTube

1. YouTube is the world's leading video service for finding, sharing and editing video.

2. The service lets you upload videos from anywhere, grab whole videos or parts to share, and create playlists and channels to collect and share information.

3. YouTube lets you edit, combine and enhance your videos with branding, annotations, audio changes and more.

4. You can make money off your YouTube collection with monetization options that allow ads before or during your video. In the past 5 years since I started posting videos, I've made a whopping 91 cents with my ads.

5. If you want to broadcast an event live, YouTube lets you plan a program and advertise to find virtual attendees.

Three Tips for Viewing or Sharing YouTube Videos

YouTube Time Sharing Option

1. View videos without ads or suggestions through **viewpure.com**.

2. YouTube makes it easy to embed and share videos, and you can even customize where you want a clip to start.

3. Make a GIF out of a YouTube clip.

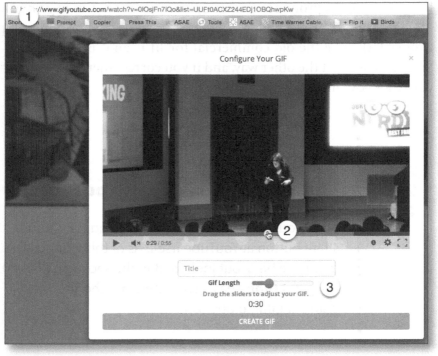

YouTube GIF Maker

1. Just type the word *gif* directly in front of the word "youtube" in the URL. You'll be taken to a special GIF-maker page—it's like magic!

2. When your video loads, move the slider to the place you want your GIF to start.

3. Then slide the Gif Length bar to the number of seconds you want your GIF to be after the starting point. When you click Create GIF, you can see and share your new GIF.

P.S.—The official pronunciation of *GIF* is with a soft *g*, as in *gem* instead of *gold*. The way I remember it is by the saying, "Choosy developers choose GIF," like the old commercial for Jif Peanut Butter. Get it? But most people say it the other way, and if you correct them, they may think you're a know-it-all nerd.

Nerd Know-How:
Easily Create GIFs from YouTube

Soon you'll be able to make a 5-second GIF through the share button at YouTube itself. As of this writing, it's still in private beta, but look for it in the second half of 2015. GIF giant **Giphy** has also gotten into the YouTube GIF game at giffffr.giphy.com.

Google Calendar

google.com/calendar

Few tools offer as much versatility as **Google Calendar**. You might consider it the building block of your time management system. The beauty of this relatively simple tool is its ability to import from, export to and integrate with an ever-increasing mountain of other apps and systems.

Google Calendar's premise is pretty simple. When you sign up for your Google account, you have a default calendar where you can add events, reminders and more. When you bring in other calendars, each can have its own color. You have all the capabilities you'd expect in a modern calendar, such as the ability to quickly add events (just type "Dinner with D.J. at 6" for an instant entry, for example), the opportunity to invite people to a meeting and the option to set recurring events.

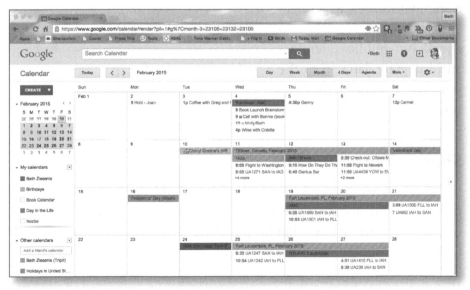

Google Calendar

Using Multiple Calendars

Google lets you add, integrate or create any number of calendars so you can see your entire world in one place. I have a number of calendars through Google, including one to track speaking engagements and one for personal events. Each one can be shared with contacts or displayed where I need it.

Add a Calendar

If you want to add a calendar from outside Google, you have plenty of options. You can add a Google calendar from a contact with a Google account or add a calendar feed via a URL in the iCalendar format, which will end with ".ics". You can also check out public calendars and integrate dates from the popular "Holidays in Norway" feed.

Add Calendar via URL

Sharing Your Calendars

My assistant needs access to my Calendar to add appointments, and my poor husband needs to see my schedule to know which city I'm in. Google Calendar makes that all possible. When you edit your Google Calendars, you find options for sharing, embedding and more.

Calendar Name:	Your Nerdy Best Friend
Description:	Events and Activities for Your Nerdy Best Friend
Location:	e.g. "San Francisco" or "New York" or "USA." Specifying a general location will help people find events on your calendar (if it's public)

Calendar Time Zone:
Please first select a country to select the right set of time zones. To see all time zones, check the box instead.

Country: United States (choose a different country to see other time zones)

Now select a time zone: (GMT-08:00) Pacific Time ☐ Display all time zones

(1) Auto-accept invitations
Calendars for resources like conference rooms can automatically accept invitations from people with whom the calendar is shared when there are no conflicting events.
Learn more

○ Auto-accept invitations that do not conflict.
◉ Automatically add all invitations to this calendar.
○ Do not show invitations.

(2) Embed This Calendar
Embed this calendar in your website or blog by pasting this code into your web page. To embed multiple calendars, click on the Customize Link

Paste this code into your website.
Customize the color, size, and other options

```
<iframe src="https://www.google.com/calendar/embed?
src=5gkpbs99bo3dei4gh6iievka1s%40group.calendar.google.com&ctz=America/Los_Angeles"
style="border: 0" width="800" height="600" frameborder="0" scrolling="no"></iframe>
```

(3) Calendar Address:
Learn more
Change sharing settings

XML ICAL HTML (Calendar ID: 5gkpbs99bo3dei4gh6iievka1s@group.calendar.google.com)
This is the address for your calendar. No one can use this link unless you have made your calendar public.

Private Address:
Learn more

XML ICAL Reset Private URLs
This is the private address for this calendar. Don't share this address with others unless you want them to see all the events on this calendar

Google Calendar Options

1. Google Calendar can help you manage your schedule without hassle—especially for invitations and meeting requests from people in your shared calendar community.

2. If you use Google Calendar to create public events, you can easily customize code to embed it in a website.

3. The Calendar Address area is where you find the URL you can share with other applications or contacts to feed your calendar where it needs to go. You can keep your calendar private or share it in a number of formats.

Nerd Know-How:
Sync Google Calendar and Outlook

Back in the day (before August 2014), Google provided a handy synchronization tool that allowed people to synchronize their Outlook and Google Calendar accounts. When Google killed the free tool (you can still find it if you pay $50 a year for a **Google Apps** account), people turned to low-cost third-party systems to keep using both platforms. **CompanionLink** is a great option (companionlink.com), as is **gSyncit** (fieldstonsoftware.com/software/gsyncit3).

3 Things to Know About Google Calendar

1. Google Calendar is a versatile scheduling tool that lets you export and import calendars to manage your work and home.

2. With Google Calendar, you can see your schedule as well as any number of other calendar feeds, from members of your family, coworkers and more.

3. Google Calendar is also a great feed to use with many third-party calendar and task apps (see Page 225).

Google Calendar Alternatives

- **Cozi**
  cozi.com

  One of my favorite calendar tools is Cozi Family Organizer. Cozi lets you set up calendars for each family member and combines them on your master calendar. You can also import other calendars, such as soccer and school schedules. The system also includes family-oriented lists to help with shopping, chores and more. Google Calendar can bring together the same types of family calendars, complete with color coding and notifications.

- **Sunrise**
  calendar.sunrise.am

  Sunrise is not really an alternative to Google Calendar: It's more the prettiest way to bring Google Calendar to your mobile devices. The interface is beautiful, and the intuitive technology helps organize your life. For example, when I use my phone to schedule a run, Sunrise automatically uses a little running guy as an icon, or a coffee cup when I set up a meeting at a café. One of my favorite features is the way you can schedule an event by dragging the selected time down the timetable. It's so much cooler than typing a time into a text field.

  In early 2015, Microsoft purchased Sunrise. We'll see where that's headed.

- **Tempo**
  tempo.ai

  I keep Tempo and Sunrise next to each other on my iPhone. Tempo also pulls Google Calendar feeds into the calendar, but then it goes a step further with predictive technology. Let's say I've scheduled a meeting with my brilliant friend Mary Byers. Tempo will send me a message to find out more about Mary before our meeting. The app seeks out her social media profiles to update me on her job position, latest updates and any other news.

NerdHerder and fellow tech speaker Sierra Modro recommends Tempo for "stalking my meeting attendees online"—in the most professional way, of course. I'm

- **Microsoft Calendar**
  outlook.com

  Microsoft has a package of free apps that are light versions of paid tools. **Outlook.com** is a cloud-based version of the Outlook we know and love (and hate a little). The Calendar works much like the regular Outlook calendar does, and you can also import and share calendars.

Nerd Know-How: Go All in with Google

Most businesses still embrace Microsoft for their operating systems, calendars, emails and Office suites. Google has a similar solution that gives you access to advanced Google integrations, extra tools and a complete Google infrastructure. You can switch your business to **Google Apps for Work** (google.com/work/apps/business) starting at $50 per user per year.

Other Google Tools

Search and Research Tools

Data is Google's prime commodity; and the service offers way, way more than just a search engine. Here are a few lesser-known Google data collections and search tools.

- **Scholar**
  scholar.google.com

  Google Scholar may make trips to the university library unnecessary. The site indexes scholarly articles and case law decisions. You can also gather the citations into a list with a couple of clicks. It's a lot easier than carefully typing out every abbreviation, comma and period like I did for my thesis. Kids today have things so easy.

- **Books**
  google.com/books

  Remember a few years ago when authors got all mad at Google because it was digitizing books without permission? My mom was a librarian, and she loved the idea of making books free for all. Google kind of backed off the concept of scanning every book, but it still has plenty in its collection, and you can search the text. Some are free as eBooks. Others have previews.

- **Alerts**
  google.com/alerts

  If you don't have time to monitor the web for important conversations, let Google do it for you. You can set up alerts for new content on a topic or term. My husband is a bankruptcy lawyer, and he receives digests of articles and posts about student loans. I have alerts set up for my name and book titles, etc.

- **Trends** and **Correlate**
  google.com/trends
  google.com/trends/correlate

  In 2008, Google started trying to predict flu activity by
  analyzing the searches related to flu symptoms. Although the
  accuracy has been questioned, the big data Google used is yours
  for the taking. You can search keywords to see trends in
  searches; and with the Correlate tool, you can see how searches
  correlate with other trends.

- **Images**
  google.com/imghp

  One of my favorite Google search tools is the image search. You
  can use the advanced features to search for images that you can
  repost without worrying about copyright. In Firefox and
  Chrome browsers, you can also drag an image to the search bar
  to find similar matches and different sizes. Plus, you can limit
  searches to a certain color or type. You can also search
  specifically for videos.

Google Search by Image

- **What Do You Love?**
  wdyl.com

  Bet you've never heard of this Google search engine. What Do
  You Love? helps you search for a term in a whole bunch of
  Google products at once.

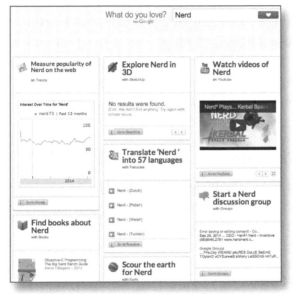

What Do You Love?

Nerd Know-How:
Increase Your Google Account Security

In the fall of 2014, Google announced support for a
security key, a special USB drive that has to be in your
computer to be able to access Google Accounts. These
start at less than $20.

Website and Merchant Tools

From free websites to analytical tools, Google has plenty of help for the online presence of your business.

- **Blogger**
  blogger.com

  Blogger is Google's free blogging platform, but I never liked the service because it linked all Blogger sites together with a "Next Blog" link at the top of your pages. I was always afraid of the blogs that might follow mine. What if I was linked to an anti-nerd site? Too risky. (See more blog tools, Page 201.)

- **Analytics**
  google.com/analytics

  You'll be amazed at the insights that Analytics can give you about your site, including real-time visitor stats, conversion rates and intricate reporting.

- **Web Fonts**
  google.com/fonts

  Want a different look for your site? Google Web Fonts helps you embed a different font family into your site.

- **Merchant Center**
  google.com/merchants

  If you sell stuff on your site, you can upload your store and product data so you show up in Google Shopping searches and more.

- **Custom Search Engine**
  google.com/cse

  Add your own Google search box to a site for custom searches to help visitors find what they need without clicking away.

- **Sites**
  sites.google.com

  Create and share a website for free.

- **Tag Manager** and **Web Designer**
  google.com/tagmanager and **/webdesigner**

  You have to really want to optimize your website to use these tools. I have no idea how to use them. Create and manage the bits of website code that help you keep stats on traffic and marketing efforts with Tag Manager, and Web Designer lets you create HTML5 stuff and animations.

- **AdWords**, **AdSense** and other marketing tools
  google.com/adwords and **/adsense**

  This is how Google makes money—big money. For a few cents a click, you can create AdWords for your business and put them everywhere. If you want to make money, you can sign up to display Google ads on your sites and more with AdSense.

- **Google Wallet**
  google.com/wallet

  This mobile app lets you organize your credit cards and money accounts and even pay with a wave of certain devices.

Security and Privacy Tools

Google is often criticized for privacy issues, but at google.com/settings, you can control what it and others can see about you.

- **Passwords and Permissions**

  Under the Security tab in Settings, you can enable 2-Step Verification, which makes you verify your identity with a code sent to your phone or email. Once you set it up, you have to create codes for access to your Google products on other devices. Two-step verification is kind of a pain, but these extra security measures may help you prevent problems.

  You can also prevent some weaker third-party apps from accessing your Google account with their possibly unsecure logins.

- **Data Management**

  You can wrap up all the data from 18 of Google's products and take it with you—including Gmail, your Blogger site, Drive and Photos—with the Takeout function in Data Tools.

- **Account History**

  This tab shows you everywhere you have been and everything you have searched for in the Google world. You can turn off Google's tracking and location services. I did this for a while, but I found that custom Google search results (even the ads) were quite handy in finding what I want.

Travel Tools

- **Flight Search**
  google.com/flights

  If you're hunting for airline tickets, Google pays attention and will search sites for you. It's as easy as typing "San Diego to DC" in the Google search box. You'll get a list of flight options and links to the airlines. Google will show a calendar of flight prices, and you may even see a notification when a flight you've searched for drops its price.

- **Translate**
  translate.google.com

  You can use Google Translate at home, but it's exceptionally helpful on the road. You can hold down the microphone and talk, and Google figures out your language then translates it. I translated the sentence "Sarah loves Hungarian goulash" into Hungarian in honor of my sister, Sarah, who definitely does NOT like Hungarian goulash.

Sarah Loves Hungarian Goulash

The app will even speak the translations for you for many languages. As of early 2015, the mobile app lets you view foreign signs through the viewfinder to see the applicable translation appear. The app has a 4+ star average review, but it's funny to read some of the comments, such as "You can find all the naughty words."

OK, maybe that's not so funny. A few multicultural activists are criticizing Google Translate for what they consider sexist and racist translations.

- **Maps**
  maps.google.com

  For quite some time, Google has ruled the world of maps. It has views from the heavens with Google Earth, and eyes on the ground with its Street View cars. This gives us the ability to see almost every detail of every location in North America, South America, Australia, New Zealand, Japan and Europe.

  This level of detail helps you get directions from almost anywhere to almost anywhere else, via public transportation, vehicle, bike or foot. It's pretty mind-blowing. Google's Map app also gives turn-by-turn directions; and it owns Waze (Page 176), which serves the same purpose but adds real-time updates from fellow drivers.

Nerd Know-How: Discover Demographic Data

In early 2015, Google Earth's Pro version for businesses and researches went from $400 a year to . . . free! Google Earth Pro helps them make business decisions based on demographics, site selection and historical traffic data. Another helpful tool is **BatchGeo** (batchgeo.com), which lets you upload lists of addresses (such as your customer database) to visualize your hottest markets.

Five Ways to Save Money on the Go

Google Flights are just one way to save money on travel. Check out these other services that can cut down on costs away from home.

1. **TripIt Pro**
   tripit.com

   As I mentioned before, the free version of TripIt (Page 170) is super awesome; but because I paid for the $49-per-year subscription, the fare-watch feature helped me get a $114 credit on Southwest when the price for my flight went down. A site called **Yapta** (yapta.com) will also track price drops.

2. **GasBuddy**
   gasbuddy.com

   Like Waze (Page 176), GasBuddy helps you find the best prices for gas in your area.

3. **Uber** and **4. Lyft**
   uber.com and **lyft.com**

   How would you like to get at least 25 percent off regular taxi rates and meet cool people to boot? Uber and Lyft are the leaders in the sharing economy's transportation options. Download the apps, and summon a car. You can see the driver's ratings, plus pictures of him and his car. The app tracks your driver's progress toward you and gives you an estimation of how long until pickup.

Most if not all of the drivers I've met keep water in the car for passengers and sometimes even snacks. One guy had Nerd Candies, as if he knew I was coming! Many drive for Lyft or Uber when they're not at a day job, though some work full time as drivers. When you arrive at your destination, you pay via the app. No more handing your credit card to a guy who uses a pencil to make a rubbing of the numbers onto a slip of paper.

5. **Airbnb**
   airbnb.com

As long as we're talking about the sharing economy, we have to mention Airbnb. This hugely popular service lets people rent rooms in other people's houses—or even the whole house or apartment. I wrote most of this book in a one-bedroom condo-type thingy in Palm Springs, California, for about $75 a night (an extraordinarily good price that I found on Priceline). I could have rented a condo from a private person in the same area starting at about $60 a night.

Although you can save money and stay cool places, I'm going to avoid Airbnb for business travel. I stayed in a young woman's studio apartment in Washington, D.C., last year; and I couldn't shower because the 8-inch black ring around the bathtub was insanely disgusting. Plus every vent in the apartment was furry with lint and dirt—yep, I said *furry*—like a squirrel had blown up in the duct system.

My hostess said, "Sometimes first-time users of Airbnb are expecting a hotel. I always try to remind them that this is just my apartment, and we do as best as we can." After the black tub and furry vents, I was ready to get back to my Hiltons.

Quick Reference Guide

• •

Organize

• •

File Storage and Sharing, 3

Dropbox

dropbox.com

Standout cloud-based storage and sharing solution

Dropbox Alternatives, 8

Box

box.com

Another cloud-based storage and sharing solution

Microsoft OneDrive

onedrive.live.com

Microsoft's cloud-based storage and sharing solution

Google Drive

google.com/drive

Google's cloud-based storage and sharing solution

Younity

getyounity.com

Cloudless storage and sharing solution

Backup Tools, 11

CrashPlan
code42.com/crashplan
Peer-to-peer backup solution

Carbonite
carbonite.com
Well-known backup service

Mozy
mozy.com/free
Another well-known backup
service

SocialSafe
socialsafe.net
Backup solution for social media
accounts

Note Taking, 14

Evernote
evernote.com
Ultimate note-taking tool

Evernote Alternatives, 20

Microsoft OneNote
onenote.com
Microsoft's note-taking tool

Notability
gingerlabs.com
App for taking notes and editing
PDFs

AudioNote
luminantsoftware.com/iphone/
audionote.html
App for recording meetings and
synchronizing notes

LectureNotes
acadoid.com
App that synchronizes notes
with audio recordings

Evernote Tools, 22

Skitch

evernote.com/skitch

Evernote's screencapture tool for computers and mobile devices

Penultimate

evernote.com/penultimate

Evernote's handwriting app

Scannable

evernote.com/products/scannabl

Evernote's document and business card scanner

Evernote Food

evernote.com/food

Evernote's food and recipe tracker

Home Organization, 23

Bawte

bawte.com

Service that replaces the appliance manuals in your junk drawer and tracks warranties

Know Your Stuff

knowyourstuff.org

Home and office inventory tool

My Measures

sis.si/my-measures

App that lets you snap a picture of an object to obtain dimensions

BrightNest

brightnest.com

Scheduling tool for household maintenance and cleaning

Key Ring

keyringapp.com

Loyalty card organizing app

Automation, 25

IFTTT

ifttt.com

Multi-application automator

IFTTT Tools, 28

Do Camera
ifttt.com

IFTTT app to automate camera tasks

Do Button
ifttt.com

IFTTT app to for other stuff

Do Note
ifttt.com

IFTTT app to automate note management

IFTTT Alternatives, 30

Zapier
zapier.com

IFTTT competitor with twice the number of connected apps and services (plus a pro version)

Wappwolf
wappwolf.com

Strangely named application automator for Box, Drive and Dropbox

Social Media Tools, 31

Hootsuite
hootsuite.com

Social media account and post manager

TweetDeck
tweetdeck.twitter.com

Twitter's social media account and post manager

Triberr
triberr.com

Site that helps you find like-minded bloggers and information curators so you can share each other's content

Buffer
bufferapp.com

Another social media account and post manager

Swayy
swayy.co

Service that sends you updates on news about your key topics so you can share on social media

Password Management, 33

LastPass
lastpass.com

Password and form-filling manager with robust free version and $12 pro level

LastPass Alternatives, 38

KeePass
keepass.info

Open-source password manager that you can store locally instead of in the cloud

Dashlane
dashlane.com

Another password manager

RoboForm
roboform.com

Form-filling service that also offers password management

1Password
agilebits.com/onepassword

Another password manager

Keeper
keepersecurity.com

Password manager and digital vault

Personal Finance, 40

Mint
mint.com

Money and budget manager

You Need A Budget
youneedabudget.com

Personal and professional budget manager

Moven
moven.com

Real-time budget manager

Credit Karma
creditkarma.com

Site that monitors your credit score and gives it to you for free

Collaborate

∙∙

Project Management, 44

Trello
trello.com
Hip service to manage individual and group tasks and projects with cards

Trello Alternatives, 48

Basecamp
basecamp.com
Grandfather of project management systems

Asana
asana.com
Slick project and task management system

Podio
podio.com
Project management system with customizable processes

Smartsheet
smartsheet.com
Spreadsheet templates with advanced features designed for project management

Task Managers, 50

Wunderlist
wunderlist.com
Award-winning task management system

Todoist
todoist.com
My assistant's favorite task management system

Redbooth
redbooth.com
Collaboration and task management tool with Gmail integration

Schedule Management, 53

ScheduleOnce
scheduleonce.com

Sophisticated system for finding a time to meet and letting people set appointments on your calendar

ScheduleOnce Alternatives, 55

Doodle
doodle.com

Simple calendar tool to let groups find a time to meet

WhenIsGood
whenisgood.net

Similar to ScheduleOnce, but not as modern looking

TimeTrade
timetrade.com

Service that lets people set appointments on your calendar

Calendly
calendly.com

Marketing Technologist Stewart Rogers' favorite calendaring tool

CRMs, 59

Salesforce
salesforce.com

Pioneering CRM that was one of the earliest cloud-based service

Contactually
contactually.com

Modern CRM with fun contact-sorting bucket game

Nimble
nimble.com

Social CRM to keep track of contacts and leads via social media and more

Charlie
charlieapp.com

Service that scans your upcoming meetings and sends you short briefings on attendees

Screensharing, 63

Join.me
join.me
Instant screensharing tool

Other Stuff

Google Remote, 66
Chrome, iOS and Google Play stores
App and browser add-on that lets
you access computers remotely

Videoconferencing, 67

Zoom
zoom.us
Impressive videoconferencing tool
with screensharing, recording and
more

Zoom Alternatives, 71

Google Hangouts
google.com/hangouts
Free videoconferencing and
screensharing tool from Google with
livestreaming options for YouTube

Skype
skype.com
Traditional video- and
audioconferencing service now
with instant language translations

AnyMeeting
anymeeting.com
Screensharing tool for small group
with robust free options

WebEx
webex.com
Webinar and online meeting tool

GoToMeeting
gotomeeting.com
Webinar and online meeting tool

Teleconferencing, 73

UberConference
uberconference.com

Innovative teleconference tool with sharing and collaboration

Speek
speek.com

(More expensive) innovative teleconference tool with sharing and collaboration

Internet and Computer Checkers, 74

Hotel WiFi Test
hotelwifitest.com

Great place to find out which hotels have the fastest Wi-Fi

Down for Everyone or Just Me
downforeveryoneorjustme.com

Handy site to check to see if a site is down

Speedtest.net
speedtest.net

Useful utility for checking Internet connection speeds

Pingtest.net
pingtest.net

Another Internet speed utility

SupportDetails.com
supportdetails.com

Site that magically loads all the details about your device when you visit

Other Stuff

Reflector App, 70
airsquirrels.com/reflector

Software that displays your mobile device on your desktop screen

Padlet, 75
padlet.com

Online bulletin board for collaborating, file sharing and content collection

Share

● ●

Screencaptures, 78

Jing
techsmith.com/jing.html
Quick and free screencapture and
screencast tool

Jing Alternatives, 83

M8 Apps
m8sftware.com
Suite of PC tools to help organize
information, clip screenshots and
more

FastStone Capture
faststone.org
Screencapture tool for PCs

Windows Snipping Tool
Windows Operating System
Windows built-in screencapture tool

QuickTime
apple.com/quicktime
Video player and recorder; Mac
version has screencapture tools

Screencast-O-Matic
screencast-o-matic.com
Another screencapture tool

PDF Management, 85

Adobe Reader
get.adobe.com/reader
Surprisingly helpful free PDF
reader with commenting and
signing features

Adobe Reader Alternatives, 87

Nitro Reader
gonitro.com/pdf-reader
Robust PDF reader with bonus tools

iAnnotate
branchfire.com/
iannotate#makepaperjealous
App for editing PDFs

Electronic Signature Tools, 88

DocuSign
docusign.com
Electronic signature manager

Sign Easy
getsigneasy.com
Electronic signature manager

Paper-Saving Tools, 88

PaperKarma
paperkarma.com
App that lets you snap a picture
of junk mail to get off lists

Print Friendly
printfriendly.com
Tools to help manage ink and
paper use when printing web
pages and more

The Printliminator
css-tricks.com/examples/
theprintliminator
Another tool to help manage ink
and paper use

Other Stuff

SkyView, 89
terminaleleven.com/skyview/iphone
Stargazing iOS app

Online Magazines, 90

Issuu
issuu.com

Service that transforms regular old PDFs into flippable catalogs

Issuu Alternatives, 94

FlipSnack
flipsnack.com

Another service to create flippable catalogs

Kindle Direct Publishing
kdp.amazon.com

Ebook publishing service for Amazon

FlippingBook Software
flippingbook.com

Downloadable software to create flippable catalogs

CreateSpace
createspace.com

Amazon's print-on-demand publication service

Content Collection, 96

Flipboard
flipboard.com

Content collector and curator for desktops and mobile devices

Pocket
getpocket.com

Content organizer and collector

Feedly
feedly.com

RSS reader and content aggregator

Next Issue
nextissue.com

Subscription service that gives you access to multiple magazines

Presentations, 98

Prezi
prezi.com

Innovative PowerPoint alternative

Prezi Alternatives, 102

Slidebean

slidebean.com

Online PowerPoint alternative that helps you create an outline and transform your presentation into beautiful slides

Sway

sway.com

Microsoft's own web-based PowerPoint alternative

Projeqt

projeqt.com

Online PowerPoint alternative with live content and social media options

Keynote

keynote.com

Apple's PowerPoint alternative

Emaze

emaze.com

Web-based, Prezi-like PowerPoint alternative

Haiku Deck

haikudeck.com

Clean, minimalistic PowerPoint alternative for mobile devices and desktops

Bunkr

bunkrapp.com

Another online PowerPoint alternative with live content and social media options

Interactive Presentation Tools, 104

Poll Everywhere

polleverywhere.com

Polling tool that uses text messages and online input to give live results

KiwiLive

kiwilive.com

Interactive presentation tool with document sharing, polling and other features

Electric Slide

electricslide.net

PowerPoint alternative that lets attendees follow slides on their devices

Design

• •

Image Editing, 108

Pixlr
pixlr.com
My favorite Photoshop competitor

Pixlr Alternatives, 114

GIMP
gimp.org
Downloadable Photoshop
competitor

Adobe Shape
adobe.com/products/shape.html
iOS app that transfers pictures
and images into vector graphics
without distortion

Pixelmator
pixelmator.com
Photoshop competitor for Mac

InkScape
inkscape.org
Free vector editor

Quote Makers, 116

Behappy.me
behappy.me
Online quote maker

Keep Calm-o-matic
keepcalm-o-matic.co.uk
Keep calm maker

Quozio
quozio.com
Online quote maker

Pinstamatic
pinstamatic.com
Pinterest quote maker

Recite
recite.com
Online quote maker

QuotesCover.com
quotescover.com
Social media quote maker

WordSwag
wordswag.co
Quote-making iOS app

Over
madewithover.com
App quote maker

Other Stuff

PicsArt, 111
picsart.com

Online creative community where artists create and share beautiful images

iWatermark, 118
plumamazing.com

Multi-platform app for adding watermarks to your images

Graphic Designing, 119

Canva
canva.com

Easy graphic design tool that makes your graphics look amazing

Canva Alternative, 122

PicMonkey
picmonkey.com

Graphic design tool with Photoshop-like features

Email Blast Tools, 123

Constant Contact
constantcontact.com

Newsletter and email blast service with surveys and event management

Mail Chimp
mailchimp.com

Newsletter service with a/b testing built in and a robust free version

Royalty-Free Images, 125

123RF
123rf.com

Royalty-free image site

123RF Alternatives, 128

iStock Photo
istockphoto.com
Getty's microstock image site

Dreamstime
dreamstime.com
Another microstock image site

Shutterstock
shutterstock.com
Another microstock image site

DepositPhotos
depositphotos.com
Another microstock image site

Fotolia
us.fotolia.com
Another microstock image site

Stockfresh
stockfresh.com
Another microstock image site

Clipart Of
clipartof.com
Marketplace for clipart

VectorStock
vectorstock.com
Marketplace for vector images

CartoonStock
cartoonstock.com
Marketplace for cartoons

Free Image Sites, 129

Flickr: Creative Commons
flickr.com/creativecommons
Free royalty-free images

MorgueFile
morguefile.com
Free royalty-free images

Wikimedia Commons
commons.wikimedia.org
Free royalty-free images

Unsplash
unsplash.com
Beautiful royalty-free images

Getty Images
gettyimages.com
High-quality images that you
can embed for free

Printed Photo Services, 130

GrooveBook
groovebook.com

App that lets you choose 100 photos a month for a printed photo book for just $2.99 including shipping

Mosaic
heymosaic.com

Beautiful photo book from your mobile device images for $25

Shutterfly
shutterfly.com

Photo and image organizing and sharing site with many products for printing and gifts

Postagram
sincerely.com/postagram

App that sends postcards of images from your mobile device for about $1 each mailed

Felt
feltapp.com

Modern photo cards and accordion-style booklets constructed with pictures from your mobile device

Coupon and Sale Tools, 131

DealNews
dealnews.com

Service that collects and shares sales and discounts

RetailMeNot
retailmenot.com

Coupon site and app that alerts you to discounts as you shop

Other Stuff

Envato, 129
envato.com

Marketplace of templates, designs, images, multimedia files and more that you can buy from designers and freelancers

Fonts, 132

Dafont

dafont.com

Massive font repository with preview capabilities

Dafont Alternatives, 134

Font Squirrel

fontsquirrel.com

Another font repository with 100% free fonts for commercial use

Kevin and Amanda

kevinandamanda.com/fonts

Repository for handwritten fonts

Google Web Fonts

google.com/fonts

Collection of fonts that you can use on websites

Font Space

fontspace.com

Another font repository

Font Finders, 135

Identifont

identifont.com

Resource that helps you identify a mystery font with a series of questions

Typetester

typetester.org

Site to test out the look of fonts on the screen

WhatTheFont!

myfonts.com/whatthefont

Resource that helps you identify a mystery font with a snapshot of the font

Wordmark.it

wordmark.it

Site that loads all the fonts on your computer so you can compare and choose the best font for a project

Create

Movie Making, 137

Animoto
animoto.com

Movie maker with templates to turn movies and images into multimedia masterpieces

Animoto Alternatives, 144

Magisto
magisto.com

Movie maker that magically merges footage and photos

Flipagram
flipagram.com

Movie maker for Instagram photos

Videolicious
videolicious.com

Movie maker with voiceover capabilities

iMovie
apple.com/mac/imovie

Apple's incredible movie maker and editor

Whiteboard Animation, 146

PowToon
powtoon.com

Whiteboard animation creator with variable pricing

GoAnimate
goanimate.com

Movie and animation creator

VideoScribe
videoscribe.co

Whiteboard animation tool for mobile devices

Wideo
wideo.co

Another whiteboard animation tool

Adobe Voice
getvoice.adobe.com

Adobe's quick movie maker for iPad only

Infographics, 149

Piktochart

piktochart.com

Infographic tool with templates

Piktochart Alternatives, 153

Easel.ly

easel.ly

My new favorite infographic maker

Infogr.am

infogr.am

Another infographic maker

Teacher Tools, 154

LiveBinders

livebinders.com

Teacher tool to organize
information

Kahoot!

getkahoot.com

Fun polling and interactive
for events

Remind

remind.com

Group texting service designed for
communication between teachers,
students and parents

Glogster

edu.glogster.com

Online poster tool that's great for
student projects and reports

Wordart, 156

Tagxedo

tagxedo.com

My favorite wordart tool of all time,
but the platform is not long for this
world

Tagxedo Alternatives, 165

Wordle
wordle.net
Classic wordart tool

Tagul
tagul.com
Another wordart tool

Cloudart
cloudart-app.com
Another wordart tool

WordFoto
wordfoto.com
Wordart app

WordCam
google play store
Wordart app

Graphic Generators, 167

Photofacefun
photofacefun.com

ImageChef
imagechef.com

Photofunia
photofunia.com

Funnywow
funnywow.com

GlassGiant
glassgiant.com

Fun Photo Box
funphotobox.com

Loona Pix
loonapix.com

Luna Pic
lunapic.com

pho.to
pho.to

Photo505
photo505.com

Travel

• •

Travel Organization, 170

TripIt
tripit.com
Travel organization tool

TripIt Alternative, 173

WorldMate
worldmate.com
Another travel organizer

Travel Tools, 174

Hipmunk
hipmunk.com
Travel reservation site with a cute chipmunk and a handy "agony" filter for finding best routes

Hopper
hopper.com
Another travel reservation site, but this one has a cute bunny

FlightAware
flightaware.com
Airplane tracking site and app

SeatGuru
seatguru.com
Travel tool that helps you find THE best seats on any kind of airplane

Rental Car Alternatives, 175

RelayRides
relayrides.com
Service that lets you rent cars from strangers

FlightCar
flightcar.com
Another car rental service that lets people rent cars that travelers park at airports

Navigation, 176

Waze
waze.com
Crowdsourced navigation tool

Waze Alternatives, 179

Moovit
moovitapp.com
Public transportation monitoring
tool

AXSmap
axsmap.com
Transportation and access
information site for people with
disabilities

Alarm Clocks, 180

Sleep Time
azumio.com/apps/sleep-time
Alarm clock app that monitors your
sleep patterns and wakes you gently

Wakie
wakie.com
Weird app that lets strangers give
you wake-up calls

SpinMe
spinmealarm.com
Alarm app that makes you gyrate
and shimmy to turn it off

Nightstand
iOS App Store
Easy-to-read clock and alarm

Carrot
meetcarrot.com/alarm
Alarm app with a nasty attitude

Other Stuff

Focus@Will, 181
focusatwill.com
Subscription service for music that
helps you concentrate

Outsource

∙∙∙

Virtual Assistants, 184

Fancy Hands
fancyhands.com
Virtual assistant service with U.S.-based helpers who take small tasks off your plate

Assistance Tools, 189

Fetch
buywithfetch.com
Subscription service for personal shoppers who help you find and buy products on the go

Path Talk
path.com/talk
Feature inside the Path social media service that lets you reach out to businesses via text

Shoeboxed
shoeboxed.com
Receipt and document management service that scans and organizes printed materials as well as digital images

Assistant.to
trybetty.com
Email-based schedule setter

File This
filethis.com
System that fetches and files your monthly banking, credit card and other statements

Other Stuff

Wegmans app, 188
wegmans.com/mobile
Store app that helps you find what you need in a jiffy

Nike+ Running, 191
nike.com
Mobile tool to track your time and outes for walks and runs

Ziptask, 199

ziptask.com

Service that helps you find and manage freelancers and projects

Website Builders, 201

WordPress

wordpress.com

My favorite blogging platform

Tumblr

tumblr.com

Social media blogging platform for really hip people

Wix

wix.com

Website building platform

Squarespace

squarespace.com

Website building platform

Strikingly

strikingly.com

Service that helps you create a mobile-friendly site

Medium

medium.com

Another social media blogging platform for really hip people

Outsourcing, 192

Fiverr

fiverr.com

Marketplace of freelancers with projects starting at five bucks

Elance

elance.com

Massive freelancer marketplace For medium to huge projects

Elance Alternatives, 198

99Designs

99designs.com

Design contest site for flyers, book covers, logos and more

Freelancer.com

freelancer.com

Another freelancer marketplace

Google

∙∙

Email Management, 206

Gmail
gmail.com
Google's email system

Gmail Add-Ons, 207

Boomerang
boomeranggmail.com
Service that lets you prioritize
your Gmail inbox

Cirrus Insight
cirrusinsight.com
Salesforce add-in that connects
Gmail to your CRM

Unroll.me
unroll.me
System that lets you organize the
email you want and get rid of the
stuff you don't

Discover.ly
discover.ly
Social media stalking tool that
gives you insight into contacts
from Gmail and social media pages

Gmail Alternatives, 211

mail2web
mail2web.com
Site that lets you check your email
accounts without a program like
Outlook or Gmail

Outlook app
microsoft.com/en-us/
outlook-com/mobile
Microsoft's mobile email tool that
integrates your calendar

Video Email, 216

Eyejot
eyejot.com
Video email tool to help your
emails get attention

BombBomb
bombbomb.com
Another video email tool

MailVU
mailvu.com
Another video email tool

Talk Fusion
talkfusion.com
Another video email tool

Other Stuff

Towelroot, 217
towelroot.org
Android rooting app that helps
you super personalize your Android
device experience

Video Hosting and Editing, 218

YouTube
youtube.com
The iconic site hides a host of
video and audio editing and
enhancement tools

YouTube Tools, 223

Viewpure.com
viewpure.com
Site that shows YouTube videos
without ads or video suggestions

Giffffr by Giphy
giffffr.giphy.com
YouTube GIF maker

Calendars, 225

Google Calendar

google.com/calendar

Google's calendar tool

Google Calendar Tools, 228

CompanionLink

companionlink.com

Service that synchronizes Google Calendar and Outlook

gSyncit

fieldstonsoftware.com/ software/gsyncit3

Another service that synchronizes Google Calendar and Outlook

Other Stuff

Google Apps for Work, 230

google.com/work/apps/business

Google's deluxe suite of business apps and office tools

Google Calendar Alternatives, 228

Cozi

cozi.com

Family-friendly calendar that brings multiple schedules together

Microsoft Calendar

outlook.com

Microsoft's free calendar is embedded in its Outlook.com site

Tempo

tempo.ai

Sleek calendar app that includes social media insights about contacts plus links to past conversations

Sunrise

calendar.sunrise.am

Beautiful calendar app

Google Search and Research Tools, 231

Scholar
scholar.google.com

Google's search for scholarly articles and case law decisions

Alerts
google.com/alerts

Automatic alerts when your keywords and names make the news or blogs

Images
google.com/imghp

Google's image search lets you search by image and filter by rights, size and much more

Books
google.com/books

Google's library of digitized books

Trends and Correlate
google.com/trends

Google's metadata analysis of, well, everything, that shows trends and correlations

What Do You Love?
wdyl.com

Google's massive search engine site that no one has ever heard of

Google Website and Merchant Tools, 235

Blogger
blogger.com

Google's free blogging platform

Merchant Center
google.com/merchants

The place to go when you want your products to show up in Google Shopping searches

Sites
sites.google.com

Website creation and hosting for free

Analytics
google.com/analytics

A tool that lets you monitor every detail of traffic on your websites

Custom Search Engine
google.com/cse

A custom search engine for your site

Tag Manager
google.com/tagmanager

Advanced site optimization tool

Web Designer
google.com/webdesigner
Google's tool to create HTML5 stuff and animations

AdWords
google.com/adwords
Pay-per-click ad service that lets you get exposure through Google and partners

AdSense
google.com/adsense
Service that lets you make money from showing Google ads on your pages

Google Wallet
google.com/wallet
Mobile credit card and money manager

Google Travel Tools, 237

Flight
google.com/flights
Google's robust travel search engine

Translate
translate.google.com
Instant language translation with voice recognition

Maps
maps.google.com
Google's map tool with features such as street view and Google Earth

Map Demographic Tools, 238

Google Earth Pro
google.com/earth
Advanced demographic mapping tool that gives businesses insight into key metrics

BatchGeo
batchgeo.com
Site that processes lists of addresse to help businesses visualize customer base

Money-Saving Travel Tools, 239

GasBuddy
gasbuddy.com
Service that helps you find the lowest prices on gas wherever you travel

Uber
uber.com
Taxi service for the sharing economy

Lyft
lyft.com
Another taxi service

Airbnb
airbnb.com
Room and house rental from complete strangers

Subject Index

Subject Index

Subject Index

CPSIA information can be obtained at www.ICGtesting.com
Printed in the USA
LVOW01s2148210715

447143LV00017B/566/P

9 780692 453360